engage

Level 1

Teacher's Book

Nicholas Tims

Gregory J. Manin   Alicia Artusi

OXFORD
UNIVERSITY PRESS
Great Clarendon Street, Oxford OX2 6DP

Oxford University Press is a department of the University of Oxford. It furthers the University's objective of excellence in research, scholarship, and education by publishing worldwide in

Oxford New York

Auckland Bangkok Buenos Aires Cape Town Chennai
Dar es Salaam Delhi Hong Kong Istanbul Karachi Kolkata
Kuala Lumpur Madrid Melbourne Mexico City Mumbai
Nairobi São Paulo Shanghai Taipei Tokyo Toronto

OXFORD and OXFORD ENGLISH are registered trade marks of Oxford University Press in the UK and in certain other countries

First published 2006
2010 2009 2008 2007 2006
10 9 8 7 6 5 4 3 2 1

ISBN-13: 978 0 19 453650 9
ISBN-10: 0 19 453650 5

Printed in China

Contents

Introduction

Teaching notes

Workbook answer key

Introduction

Overview of *Engage*

Engage uses a wide range of topics to contextualize new language, combining a strong visual impact with an exceptionally clear, well-paced syllabus.
Engage is easy for both teachers and students to use. It is stimulating but not confusing; structured but not rigid; straightforward without being simplistic.
The material encourages students to truly **engage** with the process of learning English at every level.

Topics

By focusing on a different topic in each teaching unit, students use English to **engage** with the world around them. Sometimes this is through factual presentations, sometimes through fictional characters and situations – but always with the aim of teaching students about a particular aspect of the real world. A wide range of topics and formats are used, mixing cultural and cross-curricular features with more light-hearted presentations.

Vocabulary

In **Engage**, vocabulary provides the gateway to the unit topic. Each teaching unit presents two sets of active vocabulary, using a mixture of textual and visual input. Together, the topic and vocabulary set give students the tools they will need for subsequent grammar practice, and for skills work at the end of the unit. All the items are modeled on the ***Audio CDs*** for students to listen and repeat as a class.

Additional vocabulary input is provided by the ***Workbook***, where **Extend your vocabulary** exercises introduce a further set of words related to the topic of the relevant Student Book lesson.

Grammar

Engage features two single-page grammar lessons per unit. Each lesson presents and practices a single small point, rather than dabbling in several points at a time. Tenses and other complex areas of grammar are divided over a number of lessons and units. This focused, step-by-step approach makes new language more accessible and easier to digest.

Comprehensive grammar charts are given on the page, so that students have a correct model to work from at all times. Grammar practice activities are carefully graded, from recognition exercises at the start of the lesson, to sentence production at the end, with the result that students can see real progress as they work their way through the lesson.

Communication

Each grammar lesson ends with a short **Over to you!** activity, which provides the opportunity for meaningful, personalized practice in the form of a simple speaking activity. A guided preparatory stage, usually written, builds students' confidence before they speak. All **Over to you!** activities can be done either as a whole class or, if conditions allow, in pairs.

Skills

Special attention is given to the gradual, controlled development of the four skills, through a two-page **Living English** section at the end of every unit. Reading features in every unit, along with two of the remaining three skills.

From the very first unit, **Engage** aims to build students' competence in both receptive and productive skills. Simple strategies help students learn how to read and write more effectively, while speaking lessons include guided exercises on pronunciation within the context of short dialogs. For both speaking and writing, a brief, carefully structured model is provided on the page, so that students have a clear framework on which to hang their own ideas. Listening scripts and activities are deliberately short and simple to begin with, in order to help students gradually get used to recognizing the sounds of spoken English. Levels 2 and 3 build on this by introducing a series of basic listening strategies.

Learning

It is important that students learn to take control of their learning and study techniques from the earliest opportunity. **Engage** addresses this need by including study skills after every two units, as part of the **Review** lessons. These cover a range of issues – from the basics of understanding instructions in the coursebook, to ways of using English outside the classroom – and always include a follow-up practice activity.

Mixed ability

The flexibility of **Engage** makes it ideal for mixed-ability classes. An example of this is the series of vocabulary and grammar-related puzzles in the **Magazine** section of the Student Book, to which fast finishers are directed at the end of each grammar lesson. The core material itself is also easy to adapt to the needs of different groups or individuals, allowing the teacher to place more or less emphasis on listening, speaking, reading or writing as appropriate.

Photocopiable ***Mixed-Ability Worksheets*** are designed to cater for students at different stages of learning, with both support activities for weaker students, and freer extension activities for the more able students. Further suggestions for graded follow-up activities are given in the ***Teacher's Book***.

Cross-curricular content

A strong emphasis on real-world topics provides an excellent springboard for dealing with other areas of the curriculum. Throughout **Engage**, students are encouraged not just to learn a series of words and structures, but rather to use English as a tool for expanding their knowledge of the world around them. Features on music, movies and popular culture sit comfortably alongside texts about geography, history and technology. Whatever the topic, the aim is to make it informative, accessible and relevant.

In addition, the material gives numerous opportunities for reinforcing basic values and areas of general education. For instance, the importance of tolerance and respect for others is a theme which runs throughout each book, as demonstrated by the inclusion of a diverse range of nationalities, cultures and social backgrounds in the presentations and reading texts. Other areas seen in **Engage** include gender equality, consumer education, and health.

The **Unit summaries** in this ***Teacher's Book*** list all relevant values and cross-curricular subjects covered in each unit.

Extension

Engage features a wealth of extra resources, which can be used with the whole class, as extra self-study material, or as extension for individual students. Within the Student Book, the **Magazine** section provides puzzles, extra reading texts, and guided projects.

The ***Workbook*** includes two **Extend your vocabulary** exercises per unit; also featured in the Workbook are four **Extra reading** lessons, based on extracts from the ***Oxford Bookworms Library***.

The ***Teacher's Book*** includes suggestions for extra follow-up activities within the notes for each class, where appropriate.

The photocopiable ***Mixed-Ability Worksheets*** each include one freer extension exercise for more able students, as well as extra support for weaker students and a practice activity for the rest of the class.

Recycling

In each level of **Engage** the early units review and consolidate the principal areas of grammar from the previous level. Familiar vocabulary and grammar is periodically revisited and extended throughout the book, so that students are always building on what they know.

New language is constantly recycled at each stage of the course. Each new vocabulary set is immediately practiced, and then actively used in subsequent grammar lessons and skills lessons. All vocabulary sets and grammar points are systematically reviewed after every two units, in two-page **Review** lessons. In addition, the last teaching unit of each Student Book ends with a game which reviews all the structures covered in the book.

An additional resource for reviewing recently acquired language is through the **Project** pages of the **Magazine** section. The projects have been carefully designed so that students review and actively use the most important language from the previous three units.

Further practice is provided in the ***Workbook*** and ***Mixed-Ability Worksheets***.

Assessment

Photocopiable ***Tests*** provide a convenient method of assessment for both teacher and students. There is one two-page test covering vocabulary, grammar and reading, for use after every Student Book unit. Exercises are graded in such a way that all abilities of students are catered for.

Using the Student Book

Teaching units are divided into three sections of two pages each. **Exploring the topic** and **Building the topic** each have one page of vocabulary and one page of grammar; **Living English** ends the unit with two pages of skills work. The material is organized so that one page represents one lesson and teaches one point.

Exploring the topic

Vocabulary

Exploring the topic opens each unit. The left-hand page is an illustrated presentation of vocabulary related to the unit topic, but also contains enough text to show the words in context and to model the key grammar structure.

The textual input is presented in a variety of formats, but generally as captions or short extracts of text to accompany the photographs or illustrations. Although the text includes a new grammar structure, there is no active use of the new grammar on this page.

Activities vary, but there are usually two main exercises. In most cases, the first of these involves some form of labeling or matching of words to visuals, sometimes requiring students to choose the correct word to complete a caption. The answers are always recorded on the ***Audio CDs***, allowing students to hear the new words, either alone or in short phrases, and to practice saying them as they repeat.

> You may wish to play the recording twice at this point—once for students to check their answers, then a second time for them to listen and repeat. Alternatively, you could model the words yourself.

The rest of the lesson is designed to provide practice of the new words and ensure that students understand the context.

> At some point during each vocabulary lesson, students have the opportunity to listen to the complete text as recorded on the Audio CDs, at the same time as they read the text on the page. This has the advantage of exposing students to the sounds of a new grammar structure before they come to study it in the next lesson. Reading and listening at the same time also familiarizes students with the relationship between the written and spoken word in English, and gives them extra listening practice.

Grammar

The right-hand page of **Exploring the topic** formally presents the new grammar structure first seen on the **Vocabulary** page. The headings on the page describe the new language in both structural and functional terms. A more detailed explanation of usage is given in the **Grammar Summary** at the end of the Student Book, and you may wish to draw students' attention to this during the lesson.

Form is modeled using a comprehensive chart, which features sentences taken or adapted from the previous page where possible. The advantage of having a completed chart on the page is that students always have a correct reference point to help them.

Sometimes a **Take note!** box appears after the grammar chart. This draws attention to a particular grammatical detail—such as a spelling rule—which students will need in order to correctly produce the target language.

> Once students have looked at the grammar chart in the book, it can sometimes be a good idea to get them involved in filling in an "alternative" chart on the chalk board, using different example sentences. This provides you with an opportunity to clear up any difficulties with either form or meaning, using the students' mother tongue if appropriate. It also serves to highlight common mistakes.

Grammar practice is generally provided in the form of three graded exercises, followed by an **Over to you!** activity. The exercises begin with simple recognition, for example matching or choosing the correct answer. The aim is to get students accustomed to seeing and identifying the new structure, before moving on to production at the level of individual words and verb forms, and phrase and sentence-level production in the final grammar exercise.

At this point in the lesson, a **Finished?** symbol directs fast finishers to the **Magazine** section at the back of the book. Here they will find a word puzzle, brainteaser, or other fun activity which uses the vocabulary and grammar from **Exploring the topic**. You can, of course, use the puzzle as a fun activity for the whole class. Answers to all the **Magazine** activities are given within the teaching notes for the corresponding lesson.

At the end of the **Grammar** lesson, **Over to you!** gives students the opportunity to personalize the new language and exchange information in a meaningful way. A written preparatory stage builds students' confidence by ensuring that they have had time to plan what they are going to say.

All **Over to you!** activities have been designed so that they can be successfully completed either as teacher-led exchanges in open class, or alternatively in pairs and groups.

Building the topic

Vocabulary

Building the topic follows the same sequence and pattern as **Exploring the topic**. The **Vocabulary** page introduces a different perspective on the unit topic, and presents a new set of words, which are taught, modeled and practiced in the same way as on the previous **Vocabulary** page.

Grammar

The new language presented in the **Grammar** lesson is usually related in some way to the previous grammar point, for example presenting the negative or question forms of a new tense. Sometimes, a conscious decision has been made to deal with something relatively lightweight in **Building the topic**, especially in cases where **Exploring the topic** has covered a more demanding area of grammar.

Living English

The last two pages of each unit deal specifically with skills work. The left-hand page always features a reading text and related activities, while the right-hand page covers two of the remaining three skills. We recognize that different school systems and classroom conditions require teachers to place more or less emphasis on certain skills. By dealing with each skill as a separate lesson, this section of the unit gives you the flexibility to choose the material which best suits your own requirements.

Reading

Skills reading texts in **Living English** are longer than in the previous two sections of the unit. They deal with an aspect of the unit topic, with a factual focus where possible, and actively use the vocabulary and grammar of the unit. Any new vocabulary – whilst kept to a minimum – is included in the **Word list** at the end of the Student Book, and the language structures are strictly limited to what students have seen so far.

The accompanying exercises are designed to gradually build up students' reading comprehension skills. The first exercise focuses on global comprehension, while the second requires a more detailed understanding of the text.

Approximately half of the **Reading** lessons include **Reading skills** boxes, around which the comprehension activities are based. These boxes help students to acquire and practice simple but important strategies from the very first unit onwards.

In order to help students remember reading strategies, it is a good idea to review them from time to time. For example, if they have recently looked at how to use photos to predict the content of a text, it is worth encouraging students to do this whenever possible with subsequent reading texts.

All reading texts are recorded on the Audio CDs, for additional listening practice.

Listening

Listening scripts usually follow on from the topic of the reading text, and once again the emphasis is on building students' confidence through gradual exposure. There is an initial context check question, followed by more detailed comprehension questions. Scripts are short, and tasks are generally limited to recognition only, especially in the lower levels of the course, so that students are not having to decode several levels of information and write answers all at the same time. In Levels 2 and 3 of **Engage, Listening skills** boxes introduce students to some basic strategies to help with aural comprehension of slightly longer listening passages.

When doing detailed listening activities with the class, it is good practice for students to listen to the recording at least three times. Before playing the recording, give your students time to read the comprehension questions through so that they can predict the information, vocabulary and structures they are going to hear. On the first listening, encourage them not to write anything down, but simply to listen and try to get a general idea. After they have listened, give them a few minutes to try and answer as many questions as they can from memory.

On the second listening, students can check and complete their answers. If necessary, repeat this stage. The third time around, students correct their answers. You may wish to pause the CD at relevant points during the recording so that students can see exactly where the answers are given.

All scripts are recorded on the ***Audio CDs***, and reproduced in the teaching notes if not in the Student's book.

Writing

Writing lessons are based around a model text, which is carefully structured in such a way that students can follow it exactly when they produce their own compositions. A chart helps students to analyze the model and note down the important information. As a result, they are able to see which parts of the model text can be changed, before thinking of their own ideas and writing them in the second column of the chart. At this point, most students will be ready to write.

For weaker groups, it might be helpful to go through the model text together and ask students to identify exactly which words and phrases they can change to produce their own piece of writing. If necessary, write the model on the chalk board with the relevant words gapped out, so that students can write it down in their notebooks and then complete it.

In approximately half of the teaching units, the **Writing** lesson includes a simple strategy in the form of a **Writing skills** box, followed by a short practice activity. Strategies begin with things such as using subject pronouns with verbs, simple word order, and the use of capital letters for names.

Speaking

Speaking lessons provide a fun setting in which to review some of the language seem in the unit. A simple model dialog is presented by means of a short comic strip, with a different set of amusing characters appearing throughout each level of **Engage**.

After reading and listening to the dialog for the first time, students' attention is drawn to a particular area of pronunciation which is highlighted in a **Pronunciation** box. Specific examples from the dialog are given for students to listen and repeat. As a follow-up activity, there is an exercise featuring other examples taken from previous lessons or units of the book. To consolidate pronunciation work, students are then encouraged to practice the model dialog on the page.

In pronunciation exercises, the emphasis is mostly on recognition, particularly in the early levels of **Engage**. However, it may be appropriate with some groups to ask the class to repeat the example sentences for extra practice before returning to the dialog. Teenage students often feel intimidated by pronunciation activities, so it can be a good idea to repeat as a whole class, rather than asking individual students to repeat individually.

When practising the model dialog, students will benefit from listening to the recording again. One way to organize this is to stop the CD after each sentence initially and have the whole class repeat in chorus. Do this as many times as necessary for your students to feel comfortable with the dialog.

Finally, students adapt the model dialog to make their own personalized versions, by substituting their own ideas for the words in blue. An initial written stage gives them the chance to prepare before performing the dialog in class—either in front of the whole group or, if appropriate, in pairs or small groups.

Review

Engage features two **Review** pages after every two Student Book units. In Levels 2 and 3, there is a single **Review** page at the end of each unit. Each vocabulary set and each grammar point is individually reviewed. A **Study skills** section introduces students to basic strategies for organizing and taking control of their own learning.

Engage Magazine

At the back of the Student Book is a **Magazine** section, which features puzzles, reading texts **(Reading for fun)** and guided projects.

The puzzles are designed as a fun extra activity to be completed when students reach the end of a **Grammar** page. In mixed-ability classes, they can be used as a reward for fast finishers. Alternatively, they can be used with the whole class as a warm-up or end-of-lesson activity. Each puzzle is linked to the vocabulary and grammar of the relevant **Grammar** page.

Reading for fun texts are meant to be exactly that – reading for the pleasure of reading. For this reason, they are included as optional extras, and there are no questions or exercises associated with them. Students should feel free to dip into these at any time during the year. However, the language used in each text means that they are best read after every three teaching units.

There are four **Project** pages in the **Magazine** section, each designed to review – and encourage active use of – the language taught in the previous three units. They are easily adapted to suit the needs of your students. They can be completed individually or in small groups, in class or as homework.

A clear model is shown on the page, broken down into short pieces of text. Students first read the model and match each piece of text with a category or question. This helps them identify the subject of each paragraph, and the language used. Step-by-step instructions are given on the page to guide students to produce their own projects.

Project work gives stronger students the opportunity for freer writing. This is always to be encouraged, even if it results in many more mistakes being made.

The weakest students, on the other hand, will sometimes need extra guidance to follow the model and adapt it. As with Writing lessons (see above), a useful first step is to look through the model with the students and help them identify the words and information that can be changed.

Other components

Workbook

For every Student Book unit, there are four pages of extra vocabulary and grammar practice in the Workbook.

Vocabulary pages all include an optional **Extend your vocabulary** exercise. The aim is to introduce students to some new words related to the main lexical set from the Student Book. For the sake of variety, the new words are used passively in the subsequent grammar practice activities, but they are not essential.

A five-page section at the end of the Workbook features four extracts from ***Oxford Bookworms Library*** readers, along with accompanying activities written especially for **Engage**. Extracts have been chosen carefully so that they allow for a gradual transition between levels. For example, the Starter Workbook has extracts from **Oxford Bookworms Starters**; Level 1 Workbook has two extracts from Oxford Bookworms Starters, and two from **Oxford Bookworms Library Stage 1**.

The vocabulary and grammar syllabus of **Engage** is broadly in line with the ***Oxford Bookworms Library*** syllabus. As a result, students nearing the end of **Engage Starter** will be able to enjoy readers from the **Bookworms Starters** range. As they work their way through **Engage Level 1**, they will be able to make the transition to **Stage 1** readers, moving on to **Stage 2** for **Engage Level 2**, and **Stage 3** for **Engage Level 3**.

Teacher's Book

One of our principal aims in producing the material in **Engage** is clarity. We feel that the activities in the Sudent Book speak for themselves, and therefore require little explanation. As a result, the teaching notes are presented as step-by-step lesson plans. The notes for each activity simply state the aim, list the steps needed to complete the activity, and provide the answers and, where appropriate, the audio script. There are no paragraphs or long explanations on the page.

For ease of reference, each page of teaching notes represents a page of the Student Book. The overall contents and aims of the unit are given in the **Unit summary** at the start of the notes for each unit; individual lesson aims are listed at the top of each page.

Within the notes there are occasional suggestions and background notes providing extra support for the teacher. These include ideas for warm-up activities at the start of a class; suggestions for simple follow-up or extension activities, graded according to level; background notes on matters of cultural or historical interest arising from reading or listening texts; and notes highlighting particular pitfalls to be aware of when teaching a given area of grammar.

Material from other components of **Engage** is cross-referenced at the relevant point within the notes, to enable you to see at a glance what other resources are available to you. In addition, a comprehensive Workbook answer key is provided at the back of the Teacher's Book.

Audio CDs

There are two Audio CDs accompanying each level of **Engage**. The recorded material includes all the vocabulary activities and presentation texts, all skills reading texts, listening activities, speaking dialogs and pronunciation exercises.

Mixed-Ability Worksheets

One photocopiable worksheet is provided as extension for each Grammar page of the Student Book. Worksheets all have three activities, graded as follows.

The first activity on each worksheet is designed to give extra support to weaker students who might be having difficulty in keeping up with the rest of the class. This activity is always at a slightly easier level than that of the corresponding Student Book page, and requires students to simply recognize correct forms and usage. The aim is to give more exposure to the target language and increase awareness of how it works, before demanding production.

The second activity is pitched at approximately the same level as the relevant page of the Student Book, and provides extra practice similar to that found in the Workbook.

The final activity on each worksheet gives stronger students the chance to try a less guided activity than those found in the Student Book. This will often mean producing whole sentences with a minimum of prompting, encouraging students to provide their own ideas.

Tests

The photocopiable Tests booklet provides one two-page test for each teaching unit. Tests are divided into three sections: Vocabulary, Grammar and Reading.

At the start of every test, both vocabulary sets from the corresponding Student Book unit are individually tested. The advantage of this is that it gives all students the opportunity to show what they have learned. Some students find it hard to remember grammar structures, but are able to remember individual words and phrases. By testing vocabulary at the level of individual words, we play to the strengths of these students and give them the motivation to learn more.

In the second section of the test, both grammar points from the teaching unit are tested using a variety of activity types. Questions range from simple recognition of form, through guided phrase and sentence-level production, so that all levels and abilities of students are catered for. Once again, the emphasis is firmly placed on encouraging students to show what they **know**, rather than what they **don't know**.

A reading comprehension accounts for the final activity in each test. A short reading passage places the relevant vocabulary and grammar in context, and a series of questions briefly test basic comprehension. Some students may perform well on this question despite a relatively poor performance on vocabulary and grammar questions.

The total number of points per test is 50. By looking at each section of the test in turn, you will be able to gain useful insights into the strengths and weaknesses of individual students.

Audio CDs

CD 1

Track	Contents
1	Title
2	Welcome back, page 4, *be*, Exercise 2
3	Welcome back, page 5, The alphabet, Exercise 1
4	Welcome back, page 5, The alphabet, Exercise 2
5	Welcome back, page 5, Numbers 1–1000, Exercise 1
6	Welcome back, page 7, Classroom objects, Exercise 1
7	Unit 1, page 8, Vocabulary, Exercise 1
8	Unit 1, page 8, Vocabulary, Exercise 2
9	Unit 1, page 10, Vocabulary, Exercise 1
10	Unit 1, page 10, Vocabulary, Exercise 2
11	Unit 1, page 12, Reading
12	Unit 1, page 13, Listening
13	Unit 1, page 13, Speaking, Exercise 1
14	Unit 1, page 13, Speaking, Exercise 2
15	Unit 1, page 13, Speaking, Exercise 3
16	Unit 2, page 14, Vocabulary, Exercise 1
17	Unit 2, page 14, Vocabulary, Exercise 2
18	Unit 2, page 14, Vocabulary, Exercise 3
19	Unit 2, page 16, Vocabulary, Exercise 1
20	Unit 2, page 16, Vocabulary, Exercise 2
21	Unit 2, page 18, Reading
22	Unit 2, page 19, Listening
23	Unit 2, page 19, Speaking, Exercise 1
24	Unit 2, page 19, Speaking, Exercise 2
25	Unit 2, page 19, Speaking, Exercise 3
26	Unit 3, page 22, Vocabulary, Exercise 1
27	Unit 3, page 24, Vocabulary, Exercise 1
28	Unit 3, page 24, Vocabulary, Exercise 2
29	Unit 3, page 26, Reading
30	Unit 3, page 27, Listening
31	Unit 4, page 28, Vocabulary, Exercise 1
32	Unit 4, page 28, Vocabulary, Exercise 2
33	Unit 4, page 30, Vocabulary, Exercise 1
34	Unit 4, page 30, Vocabulary, Exercise 2
35	Unit 4, page 32, Reading
36	Unit 4, page 33, Speaking, Exercise 1
37	Unit 4, page 33, Speaking, Exercise 2
38	Unit 4, page 33, Speaking, Exercise 3
39	Unit 5, page 36, Vocabulary, Exercise 1
40	Unit 5, page 36, Vocabulary, Exercise 2
41	Unit 5, page 38, Vocabulary, Exercise 1
42	Unit 5, page 38, Vocabulary, Exercise 2
43	Unit 5, page 40, Reading
44	Unit 5, page 41, Speaking, Exercise 1
45	Unit 5, page 41, Speaking, Exercise 2
46	Unit 5, page 41, Speaking, Exercise 3
47	Unit 6, page 42, Vocabulary, Exercise 1
48	Unit 6, page 44, Vocabulary, Exercise 1
49	Unit 6, page 46, Reading
50	Unit 6, page 47, Listening

CD 2

Track	Contents
1	Title
2	Unit 7, page 50, Vocabulary, Exercise 1
3	Unit 7, page 50, Vocabulary, Exercise 2
4	Unit 7, page 52, Vocabulary, Exercise 1
5	Unit 7, page 52, Vocabulary, Exercise 2
6	Unit 7, page 54, Reading
7	Unit 7, page 55, Speaking, Exercise 1
8	Unit 7, page 55, Speaking, Exercise 2
9	Unit 7, page 55, Speaking, Exercise 3
10	Unit 8, page 56, Vocabulary, Exercise 1
11	Unit 8, page 56, Vocabulary, Exercise 2
12	Unit 8, page 58, Vocabulary, Exercise 1
13	Unit 8, page 58, Vocabulary, Exercise 2
14	Unit 8, page 60, Reading
15	Unit 8, page 61, Listening
16	Unit 8, page 61, Speaking, Exercise 1
17	Unit 8, page 61, Speaking, Exercise 2
18	Unit 8, page 61, Speaking, Exercise 3
19	Unit 9, page 64, Vocabulary, Exercise 1
20	Unit 9, page 64, Vocabulary, Exercise 2
21	Unit 9, page 66, Vocabulary, Exercise 1
22	Unit 9, page 66, Vocabulary, Exercise 2
23	Unit 9, page 68, Reading
24	Unit 9, page 69, Speaking, Exercise 1
25	Unit 9, page 69, Speaking, Exercise 2
26	Unit 9, page 69, Speaking, Exercise 3
27	Unit 10, page 70, Vocabulary, Exercise 1
28	Unit 10, page 70, Vocabulary, Exercise 2
29	Unit 10, page 72, Vocabulary, Exercise 1
30	Unit 10, page 72, Vocabulary, Exercise 2
31	Unit 10, page 74, Reading
32	Unit 10, page 75, Listening
33	Unit 10, page 75, Speaking, Exercise 1
34	Unit 10, page 75, Speaking, Exercise 2
35	Unit 10, page 75, Speaking, Exercise 3
36	Unit 11, page 78, Vocabulary, Exercise 1
37	Unit 11, page 78, Vocabulary, Exercise 3
38	Unit 11, page 80, Vocabulary, Exercise 1
39	Unit 11, page 80, Vocabulary, Exercise 2
40	Unit 11, page 82, Reading
41	Unit 11, page 83, Speaking, Exercise 1
42	Unit 11, page 83, Speaking, Exercise 2
43	Unit 11, page 83, Speaking, Exercise 3
44	Unit 12, page 84, Vocabulary, Exercise 1
45	Unit 12, page 84, Vocabulary, Exercise 2
46	Unit 12, page 86, Vocabulary, Exercise 1
47	Unit 12, page 86, Vocabulary, Exercise 2

Engage – Class plan

Class	Date	Time

Objectives

Anticipated problems

Materials

Stage	Estimated timing	Activity	Procedure

Homework

Engage – Teaching calendar

Objectives

Were they met?

What have the students learned?

New language? Skills?

Anticipated problems

Did any unforeseen problems arise?

How did you solve them?

Materials

Were they suitable?

Were the students interested?

Observations

Were the activities suitable?

Did the activities interest the students? Were all the students interested?

Which activities caused problems?

Which activities would you change or take out from that particular class?

Conclusions

What will be the next step in the learning process?

Engage – Student profile

Observation sheet

Student ____________________

Class ____________________

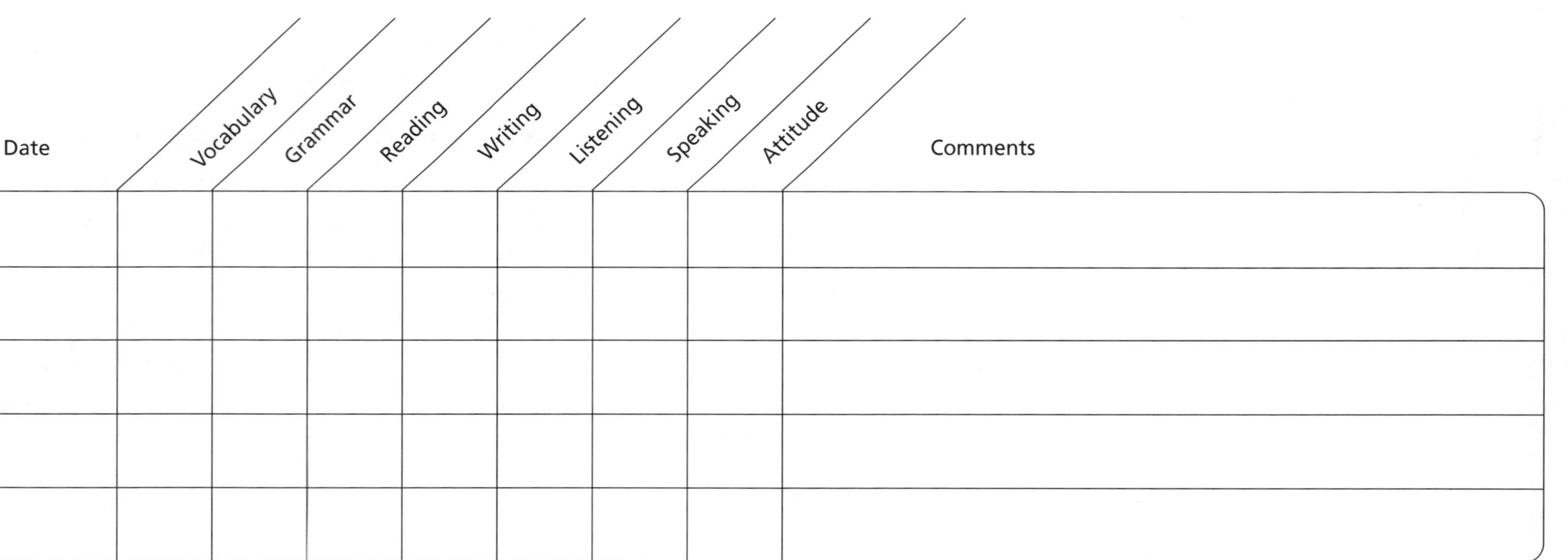

Date	Vocabulary	Grammar	Reading	Writing	Listening	Speaking	Attitude	Comments

Test results

	Date	Result
Unit 1		/50
Unit 2		/50
Unit 3		/50
Unit 4		/50

	Date	Result
Unit 5		/50
Unit 6		/50
Unit 7		/50
Unit 8		/50

	Date	Result
Unit 9		/50
Unit 10		/50
Unit 11		/50
Unit 12		/50

Engage – Self-assessment sheet

Name ____________________ Date ____________________ Unit __________

	Vocabulary	Grammar	Reading	Writing	Listening	Speaking
easy						
OK						
difficult						

Grammar and vocabulary that I need to study more:

The five most useful words from this unit were:

Engage – Self-assessment sheet

Name ____________________ Date ____________________ Unit __________

	Vocabulary	Grammar	Reading	Writing	Listening	Speaking
easy						
OK						
difficult						

Grammar and vocabulary that I need to study more:

The five most useful words from this unit were:

Contents

Reading	Listening	Writing	Speaking
oung musicians of the year eading skills: Reading for acts	Information about the actresses Emma Watson and Dakota Fanning		Introductions Pronunciation: Weak form of *can*
hat RU talking about? eading skills: Scanning	A long-distance telephone conversation		Talking about where you are and what you are doing Pronunciation: *wh*-questions
logans	My favorite basketball player: Yeo Ming	Writing a description about yourself Writing skills: Word order	
ip to Peru eading skills: Identifying parts f speech		Writing a blog entry	Talking about regular activities and what you are doing right now Pronunciation: sentence stress
ealthy eating - your way! eading skills: Reading uestions first		Writing a report about a favorite meal	Making requests Pronunciation: Weak form of *some*
creen robots	Describing two screen robots: Robby and C-3PO	Writing a description about favorite gadgets Writing skills: Word order – position of adjectives	
onsumer trivia		Writing your consumer profile Writing skills: Using paragraphs	Making offers Pronunciation: *Would you …?*
amous firsts and lasts! eading skills: Using headings	The life story of tennis player André Agassi		Giving personal information *th* sound
ammy Sosa: a baseball great		Writing about a vacation Writing skills: Commas	Talking about last summer Pronunciation: Past tense *-ed* endings
ne Piano Man: a true story eading skills: Getting the eneral idea	The life story of concert pianist David Helfgott		Talking about yesterday Pronunciation: Intonation in questions
en Trouble eading skills: Looking for key ords and phrases		Writing an email giving suggestions about what to do	Making and responding to suggestions Pronunciation: Responding to suggestions
eview			

Welcome back

Unit summary

Active vocabulary

- members of the family: brother, father, mother, sister
- the alphabet
- numbers 1–1000
- countries: Brazil, Great Britain, Japan, Mexico, Spain, United States
- days: Monday, Tuesday, Wednesday, Thursday, Friday, Saturday, Sunday
- months: January, February, March, April, May, June, July, August, September, October, November, December
- classroom objects: backpack, chalk board, bookshelf, CD player, chair, desk, door, locker, calculator, CD, folder, pen, pencil, ruler
- prepositions: in, on, under
- other: join, read, sleep, study, take, watch, work

Passive vocabulary

- nouns: apartment, break, exams, exercise, Greece, home, Peru, photo, relaxation, subject, advice
- adjectives: bad, busy, big, cool, favorite, happy, late, nice
- other: every day

Skills

- Listening to the alphabet; identifying the vowel sound in each letter
- Listening to numbers 1–1000

Grammar

- *be* (affirmative and negative)
- personal pronouns
- imperatives (affirmative and negative)

Cross-curricular

- geography

be

Aims

Review subject pronouns and *be*

1 Practice of personal pronouns

- Read the messages and fill in the blanks with the correct pronoun.
- Listen and repeat.

Answers

1 I
2 I
3 They
4 He
5 She
6 They
7 We
8 It
9 We
10 you

2 Vocabulary practice

- Look at the picture of Georgio's family.
- Label the people in the picture with the words in the box.

Answers / Audio CD 1 track 2

1 father 2 sister 3 brother 4 mother

3 Controlled practice of *be* (affirmative and negative)

- Read the text and fill in the blanks with the affirmative (✓) or negative (✗) form of *be*.

Answers

1 is
2 am
3 is
4 is
5 am
6 am not
7 are
8 are not
9 are
10 is
11 is not
12 is
13 is not

4 Read the texts again and answer the questions.

Answers

1 He's from Greece.
2 Yes, they're teachers.
3 She's from Lima, Peru.
4 They're fourteen years old.
5 Yes, he is.

The alphabet

Aims

Review the letters of the alphabet and their pronunciation

1 Presentation of the sounds in the alphabet

- Listen to the letters.
- Fill in the blanks with the letters in the box.
- Listen and repeat the letters. Then say the letters quickly.

Answers / Audio CD 1 track 3

/ei/ A, H, J, K
/iː/ B, C, D, E, G, P, T, V, Z
/e/ L, M, N
/ai/ I, Y
/uː/ U, W
/ar/ R
/ou/ O

2 Practice the alphabet

- Work in pairs. Spell the countries in the box in less than a minute.
- Listen and check your answers.
- Listen again and circle the vowels.

Answers / Audio CD 1 track 4

Br**a**z**i**l
Gr**ea**t Br**i**t**ai**n
J**a**p**a**n
M**e**x**i**c**o**
Sp**ai**n
Un**i**t**e**d St**a**t**e**s

Extra activity (all classes)

Review countries, nationality and languages

This activity can be used with any series of related words and is like a tennis game.

- Divide the class into two teams.
- One team "serves" (says) a country, e.g. *Brazil*.
- The other team "returns" the corresponding nationality, i.e. *Brazilian*.
- The first team "returns" the corresponding language, i.e. *Portuguese*.
- The teams change roles.

Numbers 1–1000

Aims

Review numbers 1–1000

1 Practice recognition of numbers

- Listen and circle the numbers you hear in each circle.

Answers / Audio CD 1 track 5

A	3,	9,	15,	13,	10
B	54,	100,	40,	30,	76
C	430,	870,	600,	320,	200

➡ **Workbook page 2**

Days and months

Aims

Review days of the week and months of the year

1 Practice of days and months

- Circle the days of the week and the months of the year in the puzzle.
- Find the two missing days and months.

Answers

V	E	J	R	Z	O	P	M	A	R	C	H	I	T
D	Z	B	C	P	S	F	T	M	I	G	S	D	H
F	S	S	M	U	A	A	L	A	L	E	E	A	U
W	E	D	N	E	S	D	A	Y	M	T	U	Y	R
N	P	D	K	Q	A	Y	E	R	E	B	T	J	S
O	T	K	O	C	T	O	B	E	R	M	E	A	D
V	E	L	P	A	U	Y	E	M	A	R	T	N	A
E	M	U	W	P	R	O	R	J	O	F	K	U	Y
M	B	K	V	R	D	V	K	U	R	R	L	A	P
B	E	A	U	I	A	E	F	N	I	I	D	R	T
E	R	J	U	L	Y	K	A	E	J	D	Y	Y	X
R	A	R	M	C	F	E	B	R	U	A	R	Y	B
J	H	C	P	A	M	O	N	D	A	Y	E	E	K

Days: Tuesday, Sunday
Months: August, December

Imperatives

Aims

Review affirmative and negative imperatives

1 Review of imperatives (affirmative and negative)

- Read the advice about you and your homework.
- Fill in the advice with an affirmative (✓) or negative (✗) imperative of the verbs in parentheses.

Answers

1 Do
2 Don't be
3 Don't study
4 Don't work
5 Take
6 Don't go
7 Don't watch
8 Read
9 Join
10 Have

Take note!

Review of imperatives

- Note the affirmative imperative is the infinitive of the verb and the negative imperative is *Don't* + infinitive of the verb.

➡ **Workbook page 3**

Classroom objects

Aims
Review common classroom objects and prepositions of place

1 Review of common classroom objects

- Label the objects in the picture with the words in the box.
- Listen and repeat.

Answers / Audio CD 1 track 6

1 bookshelf	4 door	7 desk
2 locker	5 CD player	8 chair
3 chalk board	6 backpack	

Take note!

Review of prepositions *in, on, under*

- Note we use *in*, *on* and *under* to describe the position of objects.

2 Practice of classroom objects

- Find the words in the box in the picture.
- Read the sentences.
- Write the name of the classroom object next to each sentence.

Answers

1 calculator	4 pencil
2 folder	5 CD
3 ruler	6 pen

Extra activity (all classes)

Practice classroom objects; prepositions of place

Games which require students to use their powers of observation without saying anything can be powerful ways of both quietening and motivating a class.

- Take a common object in the classroom, e.g. your pen.
- Ask students to close their eyes.
- Put the object somewhere in the classroom that will be visible to all students, e.g. under your desk.
- Ask students to open their eyes and try to find the object.
- Students write the position of the object.

➡ **Workbook page 3**

1 The other side

Unit summary

Active vocabulary

- abilities: act, dance, do martial arts, play ice-hockey, play the guitar, ride a motorcycle, speak French, use a computer
- physical appearance: eyes: big, small, blue, (dark brown), green
  hair: long, short, straight, wavy, blonde, black, (dark brown), gray, red.
  other: beard, a moustache

Passive vocabulary

- nouns: actress, CIA agent, composer, drums, language, orchestra, piano, pirate, violinist, winner
- adjectives: classical, important, recent
- verbs: tour

Grammar

- *can* (ability)
- *have* (physical description)

Skills

- Reading about young musicians
- Listening to facts about teen movie stars
- Talking about appearance and abilities; pronunciation of weak forms

Cross-curricular

- music

Values

- multicultural societies

Exploring the topic

Vocabulary

Aims
Present and practice abilities
Model *can* (affirmative, negative and question forms)

Cultural note

- **Johnny Depp** (born June 9, 1963) is an American actor. He has appeared in *Pirates of the Caribbean* and *Charlie and the Chocolate Factory*.
- **Lucy Liu** (born December 2, 1968) is an Asian American actress. She has appeared in *Charlie's Angels* and *Kill Bill Volumes 1* and *2*.
- **Kiefer Sutherland** (born December 21, 1966) is a Canadian actor. He starred as Jack Bauer, a CIA agent, in the TV series *24*.

Warm-up

Look at the pictures. Do students recognize any of the movie stars. Do they know anything about them?

1 Presentation of vocabulary set: abilities

- Look at the photos and read the sentences about the movie stars' abilities.
- Match the photos with the descriptions.

Answers / Audio CD 1 track 7

A Photo 2 B Photo 3 C Photo 1

2 Vocabulary practice; exposure to *can* (affirmative, negative, question forms and short answers)

- Look at the icons next to each sentence.
- Replace the icons with the verbs in the box.

Answers / Audio CD 1 track 8

1 play the guitar
2 ride a motorcycle
3 dance
4 do martial arts
5 act
6 use a computer
7 speak French
8 play ice-hockey

3 Identify the actors

- Read the sentences in exercise 2.
- Write the name of the actor under each description in exercise 1.

Answers

A Kiefer Sutherland B Lucy Liu C Johnny Depp

Extend your vocabulary (Workbook page 4)
Abilities: make clothes run fast swim send a text water-ski windsurf

➡ **Workbook page 4**

Grammar

Aims
Present and practice *can* (affirmative and negative)
Talk about abilities
Present and practice *can* (questions and short answers)
Ask and answer about abilities

1 Grammar chart: *can* (affirmative and negative)

Note:
- *can* is a modal verb and is the same for all persons.
- The negative of *can* is *can't*.
- We use *can* when we talk about abilities, e.g. *He can swim.* NOT ~~*He swims.*~~

See Grammar summary page 104.

2 Controlled practice of *can* (affirmative)

- Look at the ability survey.
- Fill in the sentences with the correct information.

Answers
1 30 students can play an instrument.
2 70 students can't play an instrument.
3 60 students can play a sport.
4 40 students can't play a sport.
5 82 students can swim.
6 5 students can't use a computer.

3 Grammar chart: *can* (questions and short answers)

Note:
- We make questions with *can* by swapping the pronoun and *can*. We do not use an auxiliary verb e.g. *do / does*.
- We make short answers with *Yes / No* + subject pronoun + *can / can't*. We do not use another verb in short answers, e.g. *Can you speak English? Yes, I can. No, I can't.* NOT ~~*Yes, I can speak.*~~ or ~~*No, I can't speak.*~~

See Grammar summary page 104.

4 Controlled practice of *can* (questions and short answers)

- Read the interview.
- Write questions with *can* using the phrase in parentheses.

Answers
1 Can you speak a foreign language, Jen?
2 Can you play a sport?
3 Can you use a computer?
4 Can you play an instrument?

Finished?

Fast finishers can do Puzzle 1A on page 92.

Answers

1 French	4 horse	7 dance
2 play	5 ride	
3 speak	6 ice hockey	

The hidden word is FASHION

Extra activity (all classes)

Practice of *can* (affirmative, negative, questions and short answers)

A class survey promotes language practice and allows students to get to know each other better.
- Ask students for a list of abilities, e.g. play a musical instrument and write them on the board.
- Collect enough abilities for students to choose a different ability each.
- Students ask other students in the class *Can you … ?* and record their answers.
- In feedback, write the number of students who can do the activity on the board.
- Students draw a bar chart about the abilities in the class.

Over to you!

5 Written and oral practice of *can* (affirmative and negative)

- Write six sentences about your abilities – three with *can* and three with *can't*.
- Exchange sentences with a partner.
- Tell the class about your partner using *can* and *can't*.

➡ Workbook page 5
➡ Fixed Ability Worksheets page 2

Building the topic

Vocabulary

Aims

Present and practice vocabulary of physical appearance
Model *have* for physical descriptions

Cultural note

- **Jim Carrey** (born January 17, 1962) is a Canadian / American comedian and actor. His most famous movies include *Ace Venture: Pet Detective*, *The Truman Show*, *Batman Forever*. He played the character Count Olaf in *Lemony Snicket's A Series of Unfortunate Events*.
- **Uma Thurman** (born April 29, 1970) is an American model and actress. Her most popular movies include *Pulp Fiction* and *Kill Bill Volumes 1* and *2*. She played the character Poison Ivy in the movie *Batman and Robin*.

Warm-up

Look at the pictures. Do students recognize any of characters? Do they know the films and the actors? (See Cultural note above and Cultural note on page 8.) Do they think they are good-looking? Why? / Why not?

1 Presentation of vocabulary set: physical description

- Look at the characters in the photos.
- Label the photos with the words in the box.
- Listen, check and repeat.

Answers / Audio CD 1 track 9

1 short, blonde
2 small, blue
3 short, gray
4 big, brown
5 a beard
6 long, straight, red
7 long, wavy, dark brown
8 a moustache

2 Vocabulary practice; exposure to *be* and *have* for physical descriptions

- Read and listen to the descriptions.
- Match the descriptions to the photos.

Audio CD 1 track 10

Answers

A Jack Bauer
B Count Olaf
C Poison Ivy
D Jack Sparrow

Extend your vocabulary (Workbook page 6)
Physical descriptions: good-looking curly short tall dark overweight slim bald strong

➡ **Workbook page 6**

Grammar

Aims

Present and practice *have* (affirmative and negative)
Review *be* (physical description)
Talk about physical appearance

1 Grammar chart: *have*

Note:
- We use *have / don't have* to talk about physical description, e.g. hair and eyes.
- We use *have / don't have* with *I, you, we, they*.
- We use *has / doesn't have* with *he / she / it*.

See Grammar summary page 104.

2 Controlled practice of *has / have* (affirmative / negative)

- Read the descriptions.
- Fill in the sentences with the correct form of *have* or *has*.

Answers

1 has
2 doesn't have
3 has
4 have
5 have
6 have
7 don't have
8 has
9 have
10 have

Note:
- ***have* + adjective + noun / *is* + adjective**
- We use *have* + adjective + noun or *be* + adjective to talk about a person's physical charactersitics e.g. *She has blue eyes.* e.g. *He is short.*

3 Review of *be* (affirmative and negative); controlled practice of *have / has*

- Look at the poster.
- Fill in the sentences with the correct form of *be* or *have*.

Answers

1 is, has
2 is, isn't, has
3 isn't, is, has
4 isn't, has

Finished?

Fast finishers can do Puzzle 1B on page 92.

Answers

Height: tall
Hair: long, wavy
Hair (Color): red
Eyes: big
Eyes (Color): blue

Over to you!

4 Personalization; practice of *be / have*; practice of vocabulary of physical description

- Think of a character from your favorite movie.
- Take turns to tell your partner what your favourite movie is and describe the character using the words in the box.

Extra activity (all classes)

Practice physical description with *be* and *have*.

- Students describe a person in their class and play a guessing game.
- Each student secretly chooses a person in the class.
- Students describe the person and other students take turns to guess who it is.

➡ **Workbook page 7**
➡ **Mixed Ability Worksheets page 3**

Living English

Aims

Read about young musicians.
Identify facts in a reading text quickly.
Listen and identify facts about teen film stars.
Describe physical appearance using *have* and abilities using *can*.
Using weak forms of *can* appropriately.

Reading

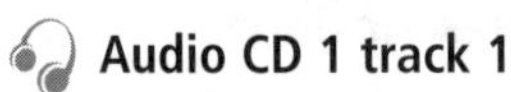

Audio CD 1 track 11

Cultural note

- **The British Broadcasting Corporation (BBC)** is a radio and television company in Britain. It was started in 1922.
- **The Young Musician of the Year** is a competition for musicians eighteen and under that is held every two years in Britain. It started in 1978. Many winners have had very successful careers in music.

Warm-up

Do any students play any musical instruments? What do they play? What kind of music do they like playing? Have they ever entered any music competitions?

1 Comprehension task (first reading)

- Read the text quickly, looking for the facts about the instruments and the musicians' ages.
- Write the words next to the musicians' names.

Answers

1	2
Nicola – violin	Nicola – 17
Benjamin – piano	Benjamin – 12
Lucy – drums	Lucy – 18

2 Reading skills

Read the reading skills box.

Reading skills: Reading for facts
Answering comprehension questions often involves looking for specific facts. It is not always necessary to read every word of a text to find facts. Practicing this skill is especially important when you need to read texts quickly, e.g. in an exam.

3 Detailed comprehension task (second reading)

- Read the text again.
- Write the answers to the questions.

Answers

1 Yes, she can.
2 Benjamin has blue eyes.
3 She's from Scotland.
4 It's brown.
5 Yes, he is.
6 Lucy can play different kinds of music.

Listening

Cultural note

- **Emma Watson** (born April 15, 1990) is a British movie actress. She has appeared in all the *Harry Potter* series of movies as Hermione Granger.
- **Dakota Fanning** (born February 23, 1994) is an American TV and movie actress. She appeared in *War of the Worlds* with Tom Cruise.

1 Comprehension task (first listening)

- Listen and write the correct name under the photos: Emma Watson or Dakota Fanning.

Audio CD 1 track 12

Emma Watson is an actress. She's Hermione Granger in the *Harry Potter* movies. She's from England. She's tall and beautiful. She has long blond hair, but she doesn't have blond hair in the *Harry Potter* movies she has brown hair. She can play hockey and tennis. She can speak French, Italian and German.

Dakota Fanning is an actress. She's Rachel in *War of the Worlds*, a movie with Tom Cruise. She's from Georgia, U.S.A. She's only ten years old in the movie. She has straight blond hair and blue eyes. She can act very well, and she can make nice sweaters.

Answers

Photo 1: Dakota Fanning
Photo 2: Emma Watson

2 Detailed comprehension of listening text (second listening)

- Read the statements.
- Listen again and circle the correct words.

Answers

Emma Watson

1 England
2 long
3 hockey
4 French

Dakota Fanning

1 U.S.A.
2 straight
3 blue
4 act

Speaking

1 First listening

- Look at the pictures and read the model dialog quickly.
- Listen and read.

Audio CD1 track 13

2 Presentation of pronunciation point

Pronunciation: Weak form of *can*

We pronounce *can* in two different ways: /kæn/ (strong form) and /kən/ (weak form).

- In the affirmative and question forms we use the weak form of *can*.
- In affirmative short answers we use the strong form of *can*, e.g. *Yes, I can*.

- Read the examples in the Pronunciation box.
- Listen to the examples and repeat, using the weak form of *can*.

Audio CD1 track 14

3 Pronunciation practice

- Listen to the sentences and circle *can* when it is pronounced in the weak form.

Answers / Audio CD1 track 15

1 **Can** you play the violin?
2 Yes, I can.
3 We **can** use a computer.

4 Dialog practice

- Practice the model dialog in exercise 1 with another student.
- Change roles and practice again.

5 Dialog personalization and practice

- Look at the words in blue in the model dialog.
- Think of some different descriptions and abilities.
- Replace the blue words with your ideas to make a new dialog.
- Practice the dialog with another student.
- Use contractions when possible.

➡ **Tests page 2**

2 It's happening!

Unit summary

Active vocabulary

- weather: It's raining; It's snowing; The sun is shining; The wind is blowing
- public activities: carry umbrellas, celebrate, dance, sing, sunbathe, swim, walk, watch fireworks
- everyday activities: babysit, do homework, get dressed, sleep, wait for the bus

Passive vocabulary

- nouns: abbreviation, appointment, dating, relationship, square, text message, texting
- verbs: pay, stand

Grammar

- present progressive (affirmative, negative and questions)

Skills

- Reading about the language used in text messages; scanning a text to find information
- Listening to people talking about what they are doing right now
- Talking about where you are and what you are doing; using intonation in *wh-* questions

Cross-curricular

- geography

Values

- ethics and citizenship, consumer education

Exploring the topic

Vocabulary

Aims
Present and practice vocabulary of weather
Model present progressive (affirmative and negative)

Warm-up

How do students celebrate New Year's Eve? Do they know any New Year's Eve traditions from other countries?

1 Presentation of vocabulary set: weather

- Look at the weather symbols in photos A–D.
- Write the correct letter next to each weather phrase.
- Listen, check and repeat.

Answers / Audio CD 1 track 16

A The sun is shining.
B It's raining.
C The wind is blowing.
D It's snowing.

2 Presentation of vocabulary set: public activities

- Look again at the photos.
- Match the verbs in the box to the photos.
- Listen, check and repeat.

Answers / Audio CD 1 track 17

Photo A: sunbathe, swim
Photo B: celebrate, watch fireworks
Photo C: dance, sing
Photo D: carry umbrellas, walk

3 Further vocabulary practice; exposure to present progressive (affirmative and negative)

- Read the sentences and look at photos A–D.
- Write the letter of the places next to each sentence.

Audio CD 1 track 18

Answers

1 D	3 C	5 B	7 A
2 B	4 D	6 A	8 B

Extend your vocabulary (Workbook page 8)

Weather:	It's cloudy	It's foggy
	It's freezing	It's stormy

➡ **Workbook page 8**

Grammar

Aims

Present and practice present progressive (affirmative and negative)
Present and practice spelling rules for *-ing* forms
Talk about things that are happening right now

1 Grammar chart: Present progressive (affirmative and negative)

Note:
- We make the present progressive with *be* (+ *not)* + the *-ing* form of the verb.
- The present progressive describes actions happening right now, e.g. *It's raining*. NOT
- We do not use *have* in the continuous form for physical description, e.g. *She has long hair.* NOT ~~*She's having long hair.*~~

See Grammar summary page 104.

Take note!

Spelling rules for *-ing* forms

We make the *-ing* form:
- of regular verbs by adding *-ing*, e.g. *blow* ➡ *blowing*
- of verbs ending in *-e* by removing the *-e* and adding *-ing*, e.g. *shine* ➡ *shining*
- of verbs ending in one vowel + one consonant by doubling the final consonant and adding *-ing*, e.g. *sit* ➡ *sitting*. Common exceptions to this rule are words ending in *-l*, e.g. *travel* ➡ *traveling*.

2 Controlled practice of present progressive (affirmative and negative)

- Read the sentence skeletons.
- Write sentences in the present progressive.

Answers

1 I'm watching a movie on TV.
2 Jude isn't doing his homework.
3 They're celebrating Tim's birthday.
4 We aren't running in the park.
5 The sun isn't shining.
6 You're singing my favorite song.
7 He's sitting in the classroom.
8 I'm not dancing the tango.

3 Further practice of present progressive (affirmative and negative)

- Look at the picture.
- Read the sentences.
- Complete the sentences with the present progressive affirmative or negative of the verb in parentheses.

Answers

1 aren't dancing
2 are playing
3 isn't running
4 isn't talking
5 is watching
6 aren't singing

Finished?

Fast finishers can do Puzzle 2A on page 92.

Answers

s	w	i	m	m	i	n	g	s
a	s	o	p	c	s	d	b	u
w	a	t	c	h	i	n	g	n
a	t	i	a	k	t	m	i	b
l	i	n	r	v	t	i	n	a
k	a	g	r	d	i	n	g	t
i	g	g	y	e	n	g	b	h
n	g	b	i	m	g	e	u	i
g	d	a	n	c	i	n	g	n
s	i	n	g	i	n	g	e	g

Over to you!

4 Personalization; oral practice of present progressive (affirmative and negative)

- Look at the verbs in the box on page 14 and in the grammar chart on page 15.
- Choose a verb and quickly draw a picture of a person doing the action.
- Show the picture to your partner.
- Take turns to guess the actions and respond appropriately, using present progressive affirmative and negative (see example).

Extra activity (all classes)

Practice present progressive (affirmative)

- Students mime an action and play a guessing game.
- Each student secretly chooses a person in the class.
- Either give students actions or ask them to think of one.
- Students mime the actions to the class or in groups.
- Other students try to guess the action.
- The student who guesses mimes the next action.

➡ **Workbook page 9**
➡ **Mixed Ability Worksheets page 4**

Building the topic

Vocabulary

Aims
Present and practice everyday activities
Model question form of present progressive

Warm-up

Ask students to think of things they do every day. In pairs, students make a list. Who has the longest list?

1 Presentation of vocabulary set: everyday activities

- Look at the people in the pictures.
- Label the pictures with the words in the box.
- Listen, check and repeat.

Answers / Audio CD 1 track 19

1 wait for the bus
2 do homework
3 babysit
4 get dressed
5 sleep

2 Vocabulary practice; exposure to present progressive (questions and short answers)

- Read the questions and look at the pictures again.
- Match the answers in the box to the questions.
- Listen and repeat.

Audio CD 1 track 20

Answers

1 At Fifth and Main Street.
2 No, I'm not.
3 Yes, I am.
4 No, they aren't.
5 She's sleeping.

Extend your vocabulary (Workbook page 10)

Present actions:	wash your face
brush your teeth	get ready for school
say "Goodbye"	comb your hair

➡ **Workbook page 10**

Grammar

Aims

Present and practice present progressive (questions and short answers)
Ask about now

1 Grammar chart: Present progressive (questions and short answers)

Note:

- We make questions with the present progressive by inverting *be* and the pronoun.
- We make short answers with *Yes* / *No* + subject pronoun + *be*. We do not use another verb in short answers, e.g. *Are you working? Yes, I am. No, I'm not.* NOT ~~*Yes, I am working.*~~ or ~~*No, I'm not working.*~~
- We do not contract *be* in short answers, e.g. *Yes, I am.* NOT ~~*Yes, I'm.*~~

See Grammar summary page 105.

2 Controlled practice of present progressive (short answers)

- Look at the picture.
- Read the questions.
- Write short answers for the questions.

Answers

1 No, they aren't.
2 Yes, they are.
3 Yes, he is.
4 No, he isn't.
5 Yes, she is.

3 Controlled practice of present progressive (questions)

- Read the skeleton sentences.
- Write questions in the present progressive.

Answers

1 Are you watching the movie?
2 Are Sam and Tim getting dressed?
3 Is Kassie swimming?
4 Are your friends waiting for the bus?
5 Are we singing a rap song?
6 Is Benny using the computer?

Finished?

Fast finishers can do Puzzle 2B on page 92.

Answers

Tom is doing his homework.
Dan and Sarah are babysitting.

Over to you!

4 Personalization; oral practice of present progressive (questions and short answers).

- Choose a verb from the unit.
- Take turns to ask questions using the present progressive.
- Respond appropriately (see example).

➡ **Workbook page 11**
➡ **Mixed Ability Worksheets page 5**

Living English

Aims

Read about language used in text messages
Scan a reading text to find specific information
Identify the general content of a text message
Listen and identify activities people are doing right now
Talk about where you are what you are doing
Use intonation in *wh-* questions appropriately

Warm-up

Do students have / use cell phones? Do they send text messages? Do they use a special language?

Reading

 **Audio CD 1 track 21**

Cultural note

- **Text messaging** is a service on most cell phones which allows people to send short messages to other cell phone users. The first text message was sent in 1992 and the service quickly became popular. In 2005, over 500 billion messages were sent. The popularity of text messaging has led to a special texting language that is an abbreviated form of normal language. Some examples include u (you), r (are) and l8 (late).

1 Global comprehension task (first reading)

- Read the text quickly looking for its general content.
- Answer the questions.

Answers

It is about special text-messaging words.
The words in the messages are spelled differently from words in normal English.

2 Reading skills; comprehension task (second reading)

Reading skills: Scanning
Scanning is when you read texts quickly to find specific information. We often scan texts in everyday life, e.g. looking for specific times or prices, and it is an important reading skill to develop in a second language.

- Read the reading skills box.
- Read the incomplete sentences.
- Read the text again quickly.
- Complete the sentences.

Answers

1 texting
2 shopping
3 aren't dating
4 walking to school

3 Comprehension task for general meaning of the messages

- Read the statements.
- Read the messages.
- Write the number of the message next to each statement.

Answers

1 4 2 5 3 1 4 2 5 3

Extra activity (stronger classes)

Practice abbreviations; exposure to "real" language

Exposure to "real" language is both motivating and useful to students.

- Write the following text messages on the board:
  1 RUOK?
  2 RU zzzz?
  3 CU 2moro
  4 Luv U 4eva!
  5 RU sk8ing l8r?
  6 This Xrcize is EZ!
  7 RU 1sty?
  8 Txt mssgng is c%l
- Can students write the full forms of the messages?

Answers

1 Are you O.K.?
2 Are you sleeping?
3 See you tomorrow
4 Love you forever!
5 Are you skating later?
6 This exercise is easy!
7 Are you thirsty?
8 Text messaging is cool!

Listening

1 Global comprehension of listening text (first listening)

- Listen and answer the questions.

Audio CD 1 track 22

Abel: Hi Katie. Are you sleeping?
Katie: Oh, hi Abel! No, I'm not. It's six o'clock here in California. What time is it in Rio?
Abel: It's ten o'clock. What are you doing Katie?
Katie: I'm watching a DVD. I'm watching *Titanic*.
Abel: Is Bart watching the movie?
Katie: No, he's reading a book. What are you doing, Abel?
Abel: I'm listening to music.
Katie: Really? Is Ray playing a video game?
Abel: No, he isn't. He's dancing. It's very funny!

Answers

Katie and Abel are talking.
Katie is in California and Abel is in Rio.

2 Detailed comprehension of listening text (second listening)

- Read the verbs.
- Listen and write the correct letter next to each action.

Audio CD 1 track 22

Answers

1 K
2 B
3 A
4 R

Speaking

1 First listening

- Look at the pictures and read the model dialog quickly.
- Listen and read.

Audio CD 1 track 23

2 Presentation of pronunciation point

Pronunciation: Questions

- Our voice usually goes down at the end of *wh-* questions.

- Read the examples in the Pronunciation box.
- Listen to the examples and repeat, copying the intonation.

Audio CD 1 track 24

3 Pronunciation practice

- Read the questions.
- Repeat the questions and make your voice go down at the end.
- Listen to the questions and repeat, copying the intonation.

Audio CD 1 track 25

4 Dialog practice

- Practice the model dialog with another student.
- Change roles and practice again.

5 Dialog personalization and practice

- Look at the words in blue in the model dialog.
- Think of some different places and actions.
- Replace the blue words with your ideas to make a new dialog.
- Practice the dialog with another student.

➡ Tests page 4

1 Review

Vocabulary

1
1 play
2 sing
3 drive
4 dance
5 act
6 play

2
1 small eyes
2 curly hair
3 long hair
4 big moustache
5 dark hair
6 slim man

3
1 blowing
2 snowing
3 shining
4 raining

4
1 babysit
2 do your homework
3 get dressed
4 sleep
5 wait for a bus

Grammar

1
1 Can you dance?
2 Can you sing a song?
3 Can you play the guitar?
4 Can you act?
5 Can you rap?
6 Can you write songs?

2
1 can
2 can't
3 can
4 can
5 can
6 can't
7 can
8 can

3
1 has
2 have
3 has
4 doesn't have
5 doesn't have
6 have

4
1 is playing
2 isn't playing, is playing
3 is singing
4 isn't reading
5 isn't making

5
1 Are the kids playing a hip hop song?
2 Is the boy singing?
3 What is the girl doing?
4 Is the man reading a book?
5 Where is the woman drinking coffee?
6 Are the kids having fun?

Study skills

Students' own answers

3 Slogans

Unit summary

Active vocabulary

- habits: eat, hate, listen, live, love, speak, teach, wear
- clothes: cap, jacket, jersey, shorts, sneakers, socks, sweatshirt, T-shirt

Passive vocabulary

- nouns: athlete, cereal, chocolate, comic, hobby, meat, newspaper, orange juice, reality show, soccer colours, shirt, slogan, style, tourist
- verbs: celebrate, smile
- adjectives: boring, electronic, smart

Grammar

- simple present (affirmative, negative and questions)

Skills

- Reading a collection of slogans
- Listening to a description of a favourite sportsperson
- Writing a description of yourself; using correct subject and verb order

Cross-curricular

- Sport

Values

- work

Exploring the topic

Vocabulary

Aims

Present and practice vocabulary of common habits

Model simple present (affirmative and negative)

Warm-up

Do students know what a "slogan" is? (A word or phrase that is easy to remember). Can students remember any famous slogans in their language or in English?

1 Presentation of vocabulary set: habits; exposure to simple present (affirmative and negative)

- Look at the pictures.
- Read the slogans and fill in the blanks with the verbs in the box.
- Listen, check and repeat.

Answers / Audio CD 1 track 26

1 A normal guy speaks, a smart guy listens.
2 We wear Real Madrid colors.
3 No, thanks. We don't eat meat.
4 I hate cereals, O.K.?
5 Life teaches you. Be patient!
6 I'm not a tourist, I live here.
7 I love rap.

2 Vocabulary practice; exposure to simple present (affirmative and negative)

- Read the slogans 1–6.
- Unscramble the words in CAPITALS and write the slogan.

Answers

1 I love Tokyo.
2 We don't wear T-shirts with slogans.
3 I hate Mondays.
4 We don't eat hamburgers.
5 I listen to pop, and you?
6 I don't speak in the mornings.

Extend your vocabulary (Workbook page 12)

Habits: drink enjoy go (to dance classes) learn like meet take

➡ Workbook page 12

Grammar

Aims
Present and practice simple present (affirmative and negative)
Talk about facts and habits in the present

1 Grammar chart: Simple present (affirmative and negative)

Note:
- The form of the simple present is the same for *I / You* (singular) / *We / You* (plural) / *They*.
- We add *-s* or *-es* to the verb for the *he / she / it* forms.
- When a verb ends in *-s*, *-sh*, *-ss*, *-z*, *-x* or *-ch*, we add *-es* to the verb, e.g. *teach* ➡ *teaches*.
- Some verbs are irregular and have their own *he / she / it* forms, e.g. *has (have)*, *is (be)*
- We make the negative form of the simple present with *don't / doesn't* + the infinitive of the verb, e.g. *I don't understand*. NOT ~~*I not understand*~~.
- *don't = do not, doesn't = does not*

See Grammar summary page 105.

2 Controlled practice of simple present (affirmative and negative)

- Read the slogans.
- Circle the correct form of the verbs.

Answers

1 live
2 speak
3 wear
4 hates
5 love
6 teaches, teach

3 Controlled practice of simple present (negative)

- Read the sentences.
- Fill in the sentences with the simple present negative of the verb in the second sentence.

Answers

1 don't eat
2 doesn't like
3 don't speak
4 doesn't read
5 doesn't listen
6 don't live

4 Controlled practice of simple present (affirmative and negative)

- Read the verbs in the box.
- Look at the pictures.
- Match the T-shirts with the verbs.
- Fill in the sentences with the simple present affirmative or negative of the verbs in the box.

Answers

1 doesn't eat meat
2 drives a bus
3 watch TV
4 love parties
5 doesn't play soccer
6 don't listen to rap

Finished?
Fast finishers can do Puzzle 3A on page 93.

Answers

HATE
LIVE
SPEAK
TEACH
WEAR
EAT
LOVE
SING
The last verb is LISTEN

Over to you!

5 Personalization; oral practice of simple present (affirmative and negative)

- Fill in the chart with information about you and a friend by writing a noun next to each verb.
- Take turns to tell the class about you and your friend.
- Use the simple present affirmative and negative.

Extra activity (stronger classes)

Practice simple present (affirmative and negative)

- Students guess an animal using information about its habits.
- Students secretly choose an animal, e.g. a dog.
- In groups or in class, they describe the habits of the animal, e.g. *It doesn't like cats. It lives in people's homes.*
- Other students try to guess the animal.

➡ Workbook page 13
➡ Mixed Ability Worksheets page 6

Building the topic

Vocabulary

Aims

Present and practice clothes vocabulary
Model simple present (*wh-* and *yes / no* questions and short answers)

Warm-up

Books closed. Do students know any words for clothes in English? In pairs, students write a list. Which pair has the longest list? Write the words on the board.

1 Presentation of vocabulary set: clothes

- Look at the pictures.
- Write the words in the box next to the items of clothing.
- Listen, check and repeat.

Answers / Audio CD 1 track 27

1 jersey
2 shorts
3 jacket
4 sneakers
5 cap
6 sweatshirt
7 socks
8 T-shirt

2 Vocabulary practice; exposure to simple present (questions and short answers); revision of possessive *'s*

- Look at the pictures again and read the interview.
- Write the person next to each item(s) of clothing.

Audio CD 1 track 28

Answers

1 Andy's friends.	4 Andy.
2 Andy's dad.	5 Andy's brothers.
3 Andy's cousin.	6 Andy's sister.

Extra activity (all classes)

Further practice of family members; personalization

A non-linguistic response, e.g. drawing, is useful to students at lower levels.

- Ask students to draw their family tree but not to show it to their partner.
- Students take turns to describe their family trees to each other while the second student draws their partner's family tree.
- Students compare their drawings.

Extend your vocabulary (Workbook page 14)
Clothes: bathing suit belt coat gloves hat sandles scarf sunglasses

➡ **Workbook page 14**

Grammar

Aims

Present and practice simple present (*yes / no* questions and short answers)
Review present simple (affirmative)
Ask about facts and habits in the present

1 Grammar chart: Simple present (*yes / no* questions and short answers)

Note:

- We make *yes / no* questions in the simple present with *do / does* + subject + verb (base form), e.g. *Do you like this?* NOT ~~*You like this?*~~
- The auxiliary verb *do / does* must agree with the subject in questions, e.g. *Does he like this?* and *Do they like this?*
- The verb is always in its base form e.g. *Does he like it?* NOT ~~*Does he likes it?*~~
- In short answers, we use the auxiliary verb *do / does, don't / doesn't* and not the main verb in the question, e.g. *Do you speak English? Yes, I do.* NOT ~~*Yes, I do speak.*~~
- We make *wh-* questions in the simple present by adding a *wh-* word (*How, What, When, Where, Why*) to the beginning of a *yes / no* question.

See Grammar summary page 105.

2 Controlled practice of simple present (*yes / no* questions and short answers); review of habits vocabulary

- Look at the picture.
- Read the skeleton sentences.
- Write questions in the simple present.
- Write short answers, using the information in the picture.

Answers

1 Does Terry like hip hop?
Yes, he does.
2 Does Julia read art books?
Yes, she does.
3 Does Terry listen to pop?
No, he doesn't.
4 Do Julia and Terry play sports?
Yes, they do.
5 Does Julia eat meat?
No, she doesn't.

3 Controlled practice of simple present (*wh-* questions); revision of *wh-* question words

- Read the answers.
- Fill in the questions, using the correct *wh-* word and the simple present.

Answers

1 What do you
2 Where does he
3 What does he
4 Why do they
5 When do you
6 How does she

Finished?

Fast finishers can do Puzzle 3B on page 93.

Answers

Sports star: jersey, sweatshirt, sneakers, socks, shorts, shirt
Pop stars: T-shirt, jacket, pants, sneakers, shoes, cap

Over to you!

4 Personalization; oral practice of simple present (*yes / no* questions) and short answers

- Read the prompts.
- Take turns to ask your partner questions about him / her and his / her family.
- Tell the class about your partner.
- Remember to use *he / she / it* forms of verbs when appropriate.

➡ **Workbook page 15**
➡ **Mixed Ability Worksheets page 7**

Living English

Aims

Read and identify the meaning of slogans
Listen and identify specific information from a description
Practice correct subject-verb word order
Use a chart to plan your writing
Write a description of yourself

Reading

 **Audio CD 1 track 28**

Warm-up

Ask students where you usually see slogans. Give students 30 seconds to think of as many places as possible. Have students seen any funny slogans?

Possible answers
walls, T-shirts, TV / newspaper / magazine advertisements, on the back of cars

1 General comprehension (first reading)

- Read the slogans on the wall.
- Choose the best description of the messages.

Answers
2 Some of the messages are serious.

2 Detailed comprehension task (second reading)

- Read the definitions.
- Write the letters of the slogans next to the correct definitions.
- Choose two of your favourite slogans and write them on your folder.

Answers

1 F	4 A
2 E	5 C
3 B	6 D

Listing

1 Global comprehension of listening text (first listening)

- Look at the photo and read the questions.
- Listen and answer the questions.

Audio CD 1 track 30

Yao Ming is from Shanghai in China. His parents live in China, but now Yao Ming lives in America. He's an NBA basketball player. He's my favorite player. He plays for the Houston Rockets, and wears a red jersey, shorts and big white sneakers. I like the team colors. I have a Houston Rockets red jacket and cap, but I don't have a jersey.

Answers

1 Shanghai in China
2 America
3 basketball

2 Detailed comprehension of listening text (second listening)

- Read the statements.
- Listen again and circle the correct option.

Answers

1 China 2 Houston 3 red 4 white 5 likes
6 cap

Writing

Cultural note

- **Gorillaz** are a band that have four fictional cartoon members: 2D, Murdoc, Nooodle and Russel. They play a variety of music styles. The band was created by Damon Albarn from the band Blur and Jamie Hewlett, the creator of the comic book character Tank Girl. The band's hit songs include Clint Eastwood, Dirty Harry and Feel Good Inc.

1 Word order in sentences

- Read the Writing skills box.

Writing skills: Word order
- In affirmative and negative sentences, we always put the subject before the verb.

2 Identification of subjects and verbs

- Read the text.
- Underline all the subjects and their verbs.

Answers

I'm	I love
I study	I watch
I go	I don't watch
I like	They're
I love	I love
I don't like	I wear
I listen	I don't wear

3 Detailed comprehension of model writing text

- Read the text again.
- Fill in the chart about with information about Kelly.

Answers

the National College
parties
big dance clubs
music concerts, Gorillaz
to hip hop and electronic music
TV
watch reality shows
jeans, T-shirts and sneakers
caps

4 Preparation for personalized writing

- Fill in the chart with information about your habits and facts.

5 Personalized writing

- Use the writing model text in exercise 2 and your information in exercise 3 to write a description about yourself.
- Reread your text and check for mistakes.

➡ **Tests page 6**

4 Another day

Unit summary

Active vocabulary
- work and leisure: build, cook, fix, fly, program, report, study
- jobs: builder, reporter, computer programmer, cook
- other: clean the school, get up, go to bed, have English class, play a video game, play soccer, ride a bike, sleep, talk on the phone, watch TV

Passive vocabulary
- nouns: archeology, barbecue, blog, discovery, engineer, flute, high school, hike, history, kid, neighborhood, plane, playhouse, restaurant, routine, save, scenery, site, snack, the news, trip, wall, university
- verbs: explain, explore, fly, rest
- adjectives: amazing, exciting, special
- adverbs: totally
- other: it doesn't work, outside

Grammar
- simple present and present progressive
- time words

Skills
- Reading an online diary (a blog) about a trip; identifying parts of speech
- Writing a blog about your daily habits and what you are doing right now
- Asking about jobs and what people are doing right now; using sentence stress appropriately

Cross-curricular
- geography, history

Values
- work, multicultural societies

Exploring the topic

Vocabulary

Aims

Present and practice verbs about work and leisure
Model contrasting uses of simple present and present progressive

Warm-up
What jobs do students' parents and family do? What other jobs do students know? Do they know a verb or phrase that describes what people do in the jobs? What jobs would students like to do in the future?

1 Presentation of vocabulary set: work and leisure

- Look at the pictures.
- Write the numbers of the pictures next to the verbs.
- Note that some verbs go with two pictures.
- Listen, check and repeat.

Answers / Audio CD 1 track 31

1, 2 study	5 fly	7, 8 build	10 fix
3, 4 cook	6 report	9 program	

2 Vocabulary practice; exposure to simple present and present progressive

- Read and listen to the texts.
- Write the names of the people in the texts under the correct pictures.

Audio CD 1 track 32

Answers

A Ha Tran	D John and Darma
B Anita Dawes	E Edith Peruvia
C Amy and Judy Smith	

Take note!
- "What do you do?" is a question in the simple present. In English, it is a common way of asking what someone's job is.
- "What are you doing?" is a question in the present progressive. It asks what is happening right now.

Extend your vocabulary (Workbook page 16)
Work and leisure: cut explain fight save sell

➡ **Workbook page 16**

Grammar

Aims

Review and practice simple present and present progressive (affirmative, negative and question forms)
Talk about regular activities and things that are happening right now

1 Grammar chart: Simple present and present progressive

Note:
- We use the simple present for regular activities, habits and facts.
- We use the present progressive for things that are happening right now.

See Grammar summary page 105.

2 Review and practice of simple present

- Read the verbs in the box.
- Read the text about Emma's routine.
- Fill in the sentences with the correct simple present form of the verbs in the box.

Answers

1 lives
2 studies
3 dances
4 plays
5 travel
6 visit

3 Review and practice present progressive

- Look at the picture.
- Read the sentences.
- Fill in the sentences with the present progressive (affirmative or negative) of the verbs in parentheses.

Answers

1 is running
2 isn't flying
3 are building
4 aren't playing
5 isn't singing
6 is cooking

4 Further controlled practice of present progressive

- Look at the negative sentences in exercise 3.
- Look at the picture again.
- Write correct present progressive affirmative sentences for the negative sentences in exercise 3.

Answers

Sue is skating.
David and Hong are playing soccer.
Dana is listening to music and dancing.

Finished?

Fast finishers can do Puzzle 4A on page 95.

Answers

1 teaches
2 running
3 study
4 a builder
5 programmer
6 flying
7 cooking
8 reporter

Over to you!

5 Personalization; oral practice of simple present and present progressive (affirmative)

- Write a verb to answer the question "What do you do?", e.g. *go to school.*
- Write a verb to answer the question "What are you doing?", e.g. *speaking* (English)
- Take turns to ask and answer the two questions with a partner.

Extra activity (all classes)

Practice of simple present and present progressive (affirmative)

Practicing simple present and present progressive at the same time helps make the difference between the two tenses clearer.

- Tell students something you are doing at the moment, e.g. *I'm standing at the back of the class.*
- Then tell students something you normally do, e.g. *I normally stand at the front of the class.*
- Ask students to write two sentences: one in the present progressive about something they are doing at the moment; and one in the simple present to describe what they normally / usually do.
- Ask a students to read out his / her first sentence.
- Other students try to guess the second sentence.
- The student with the closest guess then reads his / her first sentence.

➡ **Workbook page 17**
➡ **Mixed Ability Worksheets page 8**

Building the topic

Vocabulary

Aims

Present and practice everyday actions
Model simple present and present progressive questions
Model time words used with simple present
Model time words used with present progressive

Warm-up

Ask students to write down, in a random order, five things they do every day on a piece of paper, e.g. *get up, get dressed, watch TV*, etc. Tell students to swap their pieces of paper with a partner. Can their partner put the phrases in the correct order that they happen in the day?

1 Presentation of vocabulary set: everyday actions

- Look at pictures A–J.
- Write the correct verb under each picture.
- Listen, check and repeat.

Answers / Audio CD 1 track 33

A clean the school
B play soccer
C ride a bike
D sleep
E get up
F play a video game
G go to bed
H watch TV
I have English class
J talk on the phone

2 Vocabulary practice; review simple present and present progressive

- Read and listen the text about Binh.
- Write the letters of the pictures from exercise 1 that match each paragraph.
- Answer the question about Binh's routine.

Audio CD 1 track 34

Answers

1 E, D
2 C, H
3 A, F
4 I, B
5 G, J

3 Vocabulary practice; review of simple present (affirmative) and present progressive (affirmative)

- Read the questions.
- Read the text in exercise 2 again and write the answers.

Answers

1 He cleans the school.
2 He's playing a video game.
3 He usually rides his bike to school.
4 He's playing soccer with his friends.
5 He's watching TV.
6 He usually gets up at six.

Extend your vocabulary (Workbook page 18)

do and *make*:

do the laundry	make the beds
do the housework	do the shopping
make lunch	make a phone call

➡ **Workbook page 18**

Grammar

Aims

Review and practice simple present and present progressive
Present and practice time words used with simple present
Present and practice time words used with present progressive
Talk about when something happens or when something is happening

1 Grammar chart: Time words

Note:

- We use frequency adverbs, e.g. *usually*, *normally*, *every day* with the simple present.
- Frequency adverbs like *usually* and *normally* come before the verb, e.g. *I usually get up at 7.30.*
- Expressions like *every day* come at the beginning or the end of a sentence, e.g. *Every day I have breakfast.* or *I have breakfast every day.*
- We use other expressions, e.g. *now*, *at the moment*, *right now*, with the present progressive.
- Expressions like *now*, *at the moment* and *right now* come at the beginning or end of the sentence, e.g. *Right now I'm having breakfast*, or *I'm having breakfast right now.*

See Grammar summary page 105.

2 Controlled practice of time words in simple present and present progressive sentences

- Read the sentences and notice whether they use simple present or present progressive.
- Circle the correct time word.

Answers

1 usually	4 every day
2 at the moment	5 right now
3 normally	6 usually

3 Controlled practice of time words: *usually* and *right now*

- Look at the pictures: *A normal friday evening* and *It's a special Friday evening tonight!*
- Read the sentences.
- Write *U* if the action refers to a usual Friday evening and write *RN* if the action refers to a special Friday evening.

Answers

1 U	4 U
2 U	5 RN
3 RN	6 U

4 Controlled practice of use of simple present and present progressive with time words

- Read the sentences and note the time words used in each sentence.
- Fill in the sentences with the simple present or present progressive (affirmative or negative) of the verb in parentheses.

Answers

1 don't go out	4 is wearing
2 is having	5 go
3 wears	6 are staying up

Finished?

Fast finishers can do Puzzle 4B on page 95.

Answers

Across	Down
1 normally	1 now
4 clean	2 moment
6 talk	3 bed
7 every	5 play

Over to you!

5 Personalization; oral practice of simple present and present progressive and time words: *usually* and *right now*

- Think of someone you know.
- Write two sentences about what they normally do.
- Write two sentences about what they are doing right now.
- Take turns to tell the class about your person.
- Other students try to guess the person.

➡ **Workbook page 19**
➡ **Mixed Ability Worksheets page 9**

Living English

Aims

Read an online diary (a blog) about a trip and identify specific information
Develop dictionary skills through practice of identifying parts of speech
Writing a blog to contrast daily habits and what you are doing right now
Talk about jobs and what you are doing right now.
Use appropriate sentence stress

Reading

 **Audio CD 1 track 35**

Cultural note

- **Peru** is a country in western South America. Its population is 28 million and its capital is Lima. The official main languages are Spanish and Quechua (a Native American language of South America and the language of the Inca Empire.)
- **The Incas** were a group of people who lived mainly in Peru from around the 12th century until 1533. They made many discoveries in engineering, medicine and farming and built many cities including Machu Picchu.
- **Machu Picchu** means Old Mountain in Quechua and is a large city built by the Incas in about 1440. About 500,000 people visit the ruins of the city every year.

Warm-up

Books closed. What is the most interesting place students have been to? When / Why did they go there? Why was it interesting? Are there any special places students would like to go to? Why? What do they want to see there?

1 Pre-reading task

- Look at the photos.
- Answer the questions.
- Check answers and / or tell the class what the people are doing and where they are.

Possible answers

They're exploring Inca ruins.
They're hiking.
They are in Peru.

2 Pre-reading task

- Read the reading skills box.

Reading skills: Identifying parts of speech
Recognising parts of speech can help students:
- guess the meaning of unknown words;
- find the meaning of unknown words in a dictionary more quickly and efficiently.

3 Reading skills practice

- Read the words.
- Find and underline the words in the text.
- Write N (noun) or V (verb) next to each word.
- Check you understand the meaning of each word.

Answers

1 N 2 N 3 V 4 V 5 N

4 Global comprehension task (first reading)

- Read the questions.
- Read the text quickly and answer the questions.

Answers

1 She is an archeology student / She studies archeology. She is writing a blog about her trip to Peru.
2 They are in Peru.

5 Detailed comprehension task (second reading)

- Read the statements.
- Read the text again and write T (True) or F (False).

Answers

1 F 2 T 3 F 4 T 5 T

Extra activity (all classes)

Practice of parts of speech

Prompting students frequently for parts of speech encourages them to think about it automatically.

- Tell students to write five words (verbs, nouns or adjectives) from Units 1–4 in the book.
- Students swap their words.
- Students write the correct part of speech next to each word: N (for noun), V (for verb), A (for adjective).
- Students check their partner's answers.

Language note:
- Some words could be more than one part of speech, e.g. a verb and a noun. Examples include: *dance* (N or V), *rain* (N or V), *clean* (adjective or V).

Writing

1 General comprehension of writing model

- Read the blog quickly.
- Answer the questions.

Answers

Dani Estanza is writing.
He's in Vancouver, Canada.

2 Detailed comprehension of writing model

- Fill in the chart with information about Dani.

Answers

Name	Dani Estanza
Age	13
From	Caracas, Venezuela
Normal routines	He goes to St. Damien School. He plays music, dances and swims. He doesn't usually do sports.
Doing right now	He's writing his blog.

3 Preparation for personalized writing

- Fill in the column labeled "You" in exercise 2 with your own information.
- Use your imagination for "Doing right now".

4 Personalized writing

- Follow the model writing text and use the chart in exercise 2.
- Write your own blog entry.

Speaking

1 First listening

- Look at the pictures and read the model dialogs quickly.
- Listen and read.

Audio CD 1 track 36

2 Presentation of pronunciation point

Pronunciation: Sentence stress
- In a sentence, we stress the words that carry the most information. These words include the main verb.

- Read the example sentences.
- Listen and repeat, copying the stress pattern.

Audio CD 1 track 37

3 Pronunciation practice

- Read the sentences.
- Identify and underline the main verbs.
- Listen, check and repeat

Answers / Audio CD 1 track 38

1 He **gets** up at six.
2 She usually **talks** on the phone.
3 They're **eating** Chinese food.
4 She's **talking** to her friends.

4 Dialog practice

- Practice the model dialogs with another student.
- Change roles and practice again.

5 Dialog personalization and practice

- Look at the words in blue in the model dialog.
- Think of some different jobs and what people do in the jobs.
- Replace the blue words with your ideas to make a new dialog.
- Practice the dialog with another student.

➡ **Tests page 8**

2 Review

Vocabulary

1
1 teach
2 love
3 listen
4 live
5 watch
6 hate
7 speak
8 eat

2
1 jersey
2 cap
3 T-shirt
4 shorts
5 sneakers
6 socks
7 sweatshirt
8 jacket

3
1 report
2 program
3 build
4 cook
5 fly
6 study

4
1 get up
2 ride
3 have
4 play
5 go
6 sleep

Grammar

1
1 Jill likes jeans. She doesn't like dresses.
2 Kyle and Deb listen to hip hop. They don't listen to jazz
3 You ride your bike. You don't take the bus.
4 Damon sings rap. He doesn't dance.
5 We study English. We don't study Latin.

2
1 Jill
2 Do Kyle and Deb
3 do I
4 does Damon
5 Do we

3
1 She is working. / She goes skiing.
2 They are building a house. / They drive race cars.
3 He is cooking. / He surfs.
4 They are studying math. / They dance.
5 She is teaching. / She swims.

4 Column 1: simple present
Column 2: present progressive

1 Geraldo goes to school every day.
2 He normally has six classes.
3 He usually enjoys science class.
4 Right now he is going on a trip with his science class.
5 Right now Geraldo is reading about dinosaurs.
6 Now they are walking into the science museum.

Study skills

1
1 Spelling: I really like this music!
2 Grammar: I am doing my homework right now.
3 Word Order: Do you go to school at eight o'clock?
4 Wrong Word: I read the newspaper every day.

2 Students' own answers

5 Have some more

Unit summary

Active vocabulary

- things in a restaurant: bottle, chair, glass, insect, menu, napkin, person, plate, table, waiter
- food and drink: apple, banana, bread, cheese, coffee, French fries, ketchup, oil, salt, sausages, soda, water

Passive vocabulary

- nouns: apple pie, bowl, burger, butter, celebration, corn, carrots, fast food, floor, fruit, ice cream, idea, litre, map, milk, nuts, potato chips, pumpkin pie, salad, sandwich, smell, soft drink, Swiss cheese, taste, Thanksgiving dinner, turkey, vegetable
- verbs: remember
- adjectives: gross, fresh, healthy, nasty, popular, strange, tasty,

Grammar

- *there is / there are* + countable nouns
- uncountable nouns

Skills

- Reading advice about sensible eating habits; reading questions before reading for detail
- Writing a report about favourite food
- Making requests for some food; expressing opinions on food; practicing weak forms of *some*

Cross-curricular

- science

Values

- health, consumer education

Exploring the topic

Vocabulary

Aims

Present and practice things in a restaurant
Model *there is / there are* + countable nouns

Warm-up

Books closed. How often do students go to a restaurant? What kinds of restaurants do they go to? What are their favorite types of restaurants? In pairs, give students a minute to write a list of things they would see in a restaurant. Which pair has the longest list?

1 Presentation of vocabulary set: things in a restaurant

- Look at the picture.
- Write the letters of the items next to the words in the box.
- Listen, check and repeat.

Answers / Audio CD 1 track 39

1 plate
2 person
3 waiter
4 table
5 menu
6 chair
7 bottle
8 glass
9 napkin
10 insect

2 Vocabulary practice; exposure to *there is / there are* + countable nouns

- Listen to and read the dialogs.
- Write the letters of each dialog in the correct speech bubble.

Audio CD 1 track 40

Answers

Dialogue 1 C Dialogue 2 B Dialogue 3 D

3 Vocabulary practice; practice of *there is / there are* + number + countable noun

- Look at the picture again.
- Find the things in the sentences and count them.
- Fill in the sentences with *There is / There are* and a number.

Answers

1 There is one bottle.
2 There are six tables.
3 There are four waiters.
4 There are seven people.
5 There are fifteen glasses.
6 There is one menu.

Extend your vocabulary (Workbook page 20)
Kitchen objects: bowls cups fork jug knife spoon

➡ **Workbook page 20**

Grammar

Aims
Present and practice *there is / there are* + countable nouns (affirmative, negative and questions)
Review single and plural forms of *be*
Talk about quantities of things

1 Grammar chart: *there is / there are* + countable nouns

Note:
- We use *there is / isn't / are / aren't + a / an / some / any* to talk about the quantity of things.
- We use *there is / isn't* to talk about singular nouns, e.g. *There is a waiter.*
- We use *there are / aren't* to talk about plural nouns, e.g. *There are some waiters.*
- We make questions with *there is / there are* by swapping the order of *there* and the verb *be*, e.g. *Is there a chair?*
- We make shorts answers with *yes / no, + there + be*.
- We do not contract the verb *be* in short answers, e.g. *Yes, there is.* NOT ~~*Yes, there's.*~~

See Grammar summary page 106.

Take note!
a / an / some / any
- We use *there is / isn't + a / an* + countable singular nouns, e.g. *There is a chair* and *There is an insect.*
- We use *there are + some* + countable plural nouns in affirmative sentences e.g. *There are some chairs.*
- We use *there aren't + any* + countable plural nouns in negative sentences and questions e.g. *There aren't any plates.*

2 Controlled practice of *a / an / some / any*
- Read the sentences.
- Circle the correct word.

Answers
1 a 3 some 5 any
2 any 4 an 6 a

3 Controlled practice of *there is / there are* + countable nouns (affirmative and negative)
- Read the sentences.
- Look at the picture.
- Fill in the sentences with the correct form of *be* (affirmative or negative) + *a / an / some / any*.

Answers
1 There are some chairs.
2 There is a cake.
3 There are some glasses.
4 There isn't a menu.
5 There are some bottles.
6 There is a table.
7 There aren't any insects.
8 There is a waiter.

4 Controlled practice of *there is / there are* (questions and short answers)
- Look at the words in parentheses.
- Write questions using *Is there / Are there + any … ?*
- Look at the picture again and write short answers.

Answers
1 Are there any insects?
No, there aren't.
2 Are there any plates?
Yes, there are.
3 Is there a girl?
No, there isn't.
4 Is there a napkin?
Yes, there is.
5 Are there any menus?
No, there aren't.

Finished?
Fast finishers can do Puzzle 5A on page 95.

Answers
There is a chair on a table.
There is a bottle on the ceiling.
There is a glass on the floor.
There is a table on a table.
There are two people on that table.
There is a menu in a boy's pocket.

Over to you!

5 Personalization; oral practice of *there is / there are + a / an / some*
- Look around the classroom for two minutes.
- Close your eyes and take turns to tell the class about things that are / aren't in the classroom, using *there is / there are + a / an / some*.

➡ **Workbook page 21**
➡ **Mixed Ability Worksheets page 10**

Building the topic

Vocabulary

Aims

Present and practice food and drink (countable and uncountable nouns)
Model uncountable nouns in affirmative, negative sentences and questions

Warm-up

Books closed. Ask students what their favourite foods are. Do they have any unusual tastes? Write new vocabulary on the board.

1 Presentation of vocabulary set: food and drink

- Look at the photos.
- Write the number of the photos next to the correct words.
- Listen, check and repeat.

Answers / Audio CD 1 track 41

1	ketchup	7	sausages
2	cheese	8	bread
3	salt	9	banana
4	apple	10	French fries
5	water	11	coffee
6	oil	12	soda

2 Vocabulary practice; exposure to *there is / there are* + uncountable nouns

- Read the sentences.
- Read the text about the teenagers' tastes in food and drink.
- Circle T (True) or F (False).

Audio CD 1 track 42

Answers

1 F 2 F 3 T 4 F 5 F 6 T

Extra activity (all classes)

Further vocabulary practice

Correcting false sentences provides further practice of vocabulary.

- Ask students to correct the false sentences in exercise 2.

Answers

1 Tatum's brother eats French fries with oil.
2 Ang thinks green bananas are gross.
4 José's mom loves English sausages.
5 Amy's friend eats apples with salt.

Extend your vocabulary (Workbook page 22)
Food and drink: fruit juice milk
an orange salad a sandwich soup

➡ **Workbook page 22**

Grammar

Aims

Present and practice uncountable nouns in affirmative, negative sentences and questions
Review *some / any*
Review *there is / there are* (affirmative and negative)
Talk about quantity of things that we can't count

1 Grammar chart: uncountable nouns

Note:
- Uncountable nouns don't have a plural, e.g. *cheese*, *milk*, *bread*, *ketchup*.
- We use the singular form of verbs with countable nouns, e.g. *Cheese is my favourite food.* NOT ~~*Cheese are my favourite food.*~~
- Common mistakes with uncountable nouns are: *information* NOT ~~*informations*~~, *some news* NOT ~~*two news*~~, *furniture* NOT ~~*furnitures*~~.

See Grammar summary page 106.

2 Practice of countable and uncountable nouns.

- Read the sentences and look at the nouns in bold.
- Write C for countable nouns and U for uncountable nouns.

Answers

1 U 2 C 3 U 4 U 5 U 6 C 7 U 8 U

3 Controlled practice of *there is / isn't / are / aren't* + *a / an / some / any*

- Read the sentences.
- Look at the picture.
- Fill in the sentences with the correct form of *be* and the correct quantifier.

Answers

1 is some
2 isn't any
3 is an
4 aren't any
5 is some
6 are some

4 Controlled practice of *there is / isn't* + *some / any* + uncountable nouns

- Look at the picture again.
- Find the objects in parentheses.
- Write sentences with *There is / isn't* + *some / any* and the noun in parentheses.

Answers

1 There is some milk.
2 There isn't any ketchup.
3 There is some salt.
4 There are some spoons.
5 There isn't any cheese.
6 There is a plate.

Finished?

Fast finishers can do Puzzle 5B on page 95.

Answers

apple, bread, sausage, cheese, salt, oil, banana, French fries

Over to you!

5 Game; oral practice of *there is / there are* + *a / an / some / any*

- Think of a sentence with *there is / are* + *a / an / some / any*.
- Take turns to say your sentence but replace the word *a / an / some / any* with "Joe".
- The other students try to say the substituted word.

Extra activity (stronger classes)

Practice of *a / an / some* with countable (singular and plural) and uncountable nouns

Asking students to stand up for this game will help them concentrate on the game.

- Start the game by telling students about something in your cupboard at home, e.g. *In my kitchen cupboard I have some eggs.*
- Point to a student. He / She has to repeat your sentence and add an item of his / her own, e.g. *In my cupboard I have some eggs and an apple.*
- He / She points to another student who continues.
- When a student makes a mistake or can't remember, they sit down.
- Continue until one student is left.

➡ **Workbook page 23**
➡ **Mixed Ability Worksheets page 11**

Living English

Aims

Read advice about eating "unhealthy" food
Prepare to become an active reader by reading questions first
Read a description of someone's favourite meal
Write a description of your favourite food
Request food and express opinions

Reading

 **Audio CD 1 track 43**

Cultural note

- **Fast food** is food which is prepared and served quickly in fast food restaurants. The history of modern fast food started in about 1921 with a restaurant called White Castle in America, which started selling hamburgers for five cents. White Castle still has fast food restaurants all over America.
- **Thanksgiving** is an annual holiday in the United States and Canada being thankful for everything you have. It is always on the fourth Thursday in November in America and the second Monday in October in Canada. It is usually celebrated by a large dinner with friends and family and typical food includes turkey, vegetables and pumpkin pie.

Warm-up

Do students eat healthily? What kinds of foods do they try to eat? What kinds of foods do they try to avoid?

1 Global comprehension task (first reading)

- Read the titles.
- Read the article quickly.
- Choose the best title for the text.

Answers

1 Healthy Eating – Your Way!

2 Reading skills

- Read the reading skills box.

Reading skills: Reading questions

- Reading questions before reading a text makes students "active" readers and helps them find the information they need more quickly.

3 Detailed comprehension task (second reading)

- Read the statements.
- Read the article again.
- Check (✓) the statements the writer says. Cross the statements (✗) the writer doesn't say.

Answers

1 ✗ 2 ✓ 3 ✗ 4 ✗ 5 ✗ 6 ✗

Writing

1 Global comprehension of model writing text

- Read the report quickly.
- What is the subject of the report?

Answers

The report is about a favorite meal.

2 Detailed comprehension of model writing text

- Look at the chart.
- Read the report again.
- Fill in the chart with information from the report.

Answers

Name	Angela
From	Detroit, Michigan, USA
Favorite special meal	Thanksgiving dinner
When	At the end of November
What they do	They cook in the morning, and eat in the afternoon
Food	turkey, corn, carrots, salad, bread, pumpkin pie, apple pie, ice cream
Favorite food	Pumpkin pie

3 Preparation for personalized writing

- Think about your favorite meals / food.
- Fill in the chart with your information.

4 Personalized writing

- Follow the model writing text.
- Use your own information from the chart to change the text.
- Write your report about your favourite meal.

Speaking

1 First listening

- Look at the pictures and read the model dialogs quickly.
- Listen and read.

Audio CD 1 track 44

2 Presentation of pronunciation point

Pronunciation: Weak form of *some*

- In sentences, *some* is pronounced /səm/.
- Pronouncing weak forms correctly helps students speak more naturally.

- Read the example sentences.
- Listen and repeat, copying the pronunciation of *some*.

Audio CD 1 track 45

3 Pronunciation practice

- Read the sentences.
- Practice saying the sentences with the weak form of some.
- Listen, check and repeat.

Audio CD 1 track 46

4 Dialog practice

- Practice the model dialogs with another student.
- Change roles and practice again.

5 Dialog personalization and practice

- Look at the words in blue in the model dialog.
- Think of some different foods and what you think of them.
- Replace the blue words with your ideas to make a new dialog.
- Practice the dialog with another student.

➡ **Tests page 12**

6 Robotics

Unit summary

Active vocabulary
- parts of the body: arms, ears, eyes, feet, hands, head, legs, mouth, neck, nose
- opposite adjectives: cheap / expensive, fast / slow, hard / soft, heavy / light, new / old, noisy / quiet

Passive vocabulary
- verbs: carry, cost, feel, weigh
- nouns: athletic, electronic gadget, gang, kind, metal, motorcycle, muscles, policeman, recording studio, sound effects, skater, surfboard, uniform, weight, wheel
- adjectives: alternative, flashing, human, portable, scary, smart, strong
- other: inside

Grammar
- *Whose … ?*
- possessive pronouns
- adjective position

Skills
- Reading about robots in films and TV programs
- Listening to descriptions of two robots
- Writing a description of your favourite gadgets; understanding position of adjectives

Cross-curricular
- science, IT

Values
- health

Exploring the topic

Vocabulary

Aims

Present and practice parts of the body
Model questions with *whose* and possessive pronouns
Review regular and irregular plurals

Warm-up

Books closed. Draw a body on the board and elicit words from students to label the body.

1 Presentation of vocabulary set: parts of the body

- Look at the pictures and read the questions.
- Fill in the questions with the parts of the body in the box.
- Listen, check and repeat.

Audio CD 1 track 47

Answers

1	ears	6	arms
2	hands	7	legs
3	eyes	8	feet
4	mouth	9	nose
5	neck	10	head

Take note!

Regular and irregular plurals

Regular plurals are usually formed by adding:
- *-s*, e.g. *hand* ➡ *hands*
- *-es*, e.g. *class* ➡ *classes*
- *-ies*, e.g. *body* ➡ *bodies*

There are no rules for irregular plurals and they must be learned separately, e.g. *foot* ➡ *feet*, *person* ➡ *people*.

2 Vocabulary practice; exposure to *Whose … ?* + possessive pronouns

- Read the sentences and look at the picture.
- Circle T (True) or F (False).

Answers

1 T 2 T 3 F 4 F 5 T 6 T

Extend your vocabulary (Workbook page 24)

Parts of the body: eyebrow fingers lips nails teeth thumb

➡ **Workbook page 24**

Grammar

Aims

Present and practice *Whose... ?* + possessive pronouns
Talk about things we possess

1 Grammar chart: *Whose ... ?* + possessive pronouns

Note:

- We use *Whose ... ?* to ask who something belongs to.
- If the noun is singular or uncountable, the verb is also singular, e.g. *Whose bag is this? Whose money is this?*
- If the noun is plural, the verb is also plural, e.g. *Whose shoes are these?*
- We can use possessive pronouns when the noun is obvious from the context, e.g. *Whose CD is this? It's mine. = It's my CD.*

See Grammar summary page 106.

2 Controlled practice of possessive pronouns

- Read the sentences.
- Look at the picture.
- Circle the correct possessive pronoun.

Answers

1 his
2 hers
3 their
4 yours

3 Controlled practice of possessive pronouns

- Look at the people's clothes in the picture in exercise 2.
- Read the sentences.
- Rewrite the sentences.

Answers

1 his
2 hers
3 theirs
4 Yours

4 Controlled practice of *Whose ... ?* and possessive pronouns

- Read the questions and answers.
- Fill in the questions and answers.

Answers

1 Whose, is this, It's his.
2 Whose, is this, hers
3 Whose, is this, It's ours.
4 Whose, are these, They're mine.
5 Whose, is this, It's theirs.
6 Whose, are they, They're yours.

Finished?

Fast finishers can do Puzzle 6A on page 96.

Answers

THE ROBOT CAN CLEAN THE HOUSE

Over to you!

5 Personalization; oral practice of *Whose ... ?* and possessive pronouns.

- Collect a few objects from different students in the class.
- Put them on the desk and ask questions with *Whose ... ?*
- Students take turns to guess whose object is it.

➡ Workbook page 25
➡ Mixed Ability Worksheets page 12

Building the topic

Vocabulary

Aims

Present and practice adjectives and their opposites
Model *be* + adjective possession

Warm-up

Books closed. Write the letters a–z on the board. In pairs, students try to write one adjective beginning with each letter, from a–z. Give students two minutes to write as many words as possible. Which pair has the longest list?

1 Presentation of vocabulary set: opposite adjectives; exposure to the grammar of adjective position

- Look at the pictures.
- Read the descriptions.
- Fill in the descriptions with the correct pair of adjective opposites from exercise 1.
- Listen, check and repeat.

Answers / Audio CD 1 track 48

1 It's light. It isn't heavy.
2 It's new. It isn't old.
3 It's fast. It isn't slow.
4 They're soft. They aren't hard.
5 It's quiet. It isn't noisy.
6 It's cheap. It isn't expensive.

2 Vocabulary practice; exposure to the grammar of adjective position

- Read the sentences.
- Fill in the sentences with adjectives from exercise 1.

Answers

1 noisy
2 hard
3 slow
4 expensive
5 heavy
6 old

Extend your vocabulary (Workbook page 26)

Opposites: beautiful boring difficult ugly dry easy hard-working interesting lazy wet

➡ **Workbook page 26**

Grammar

Aims
Present and practice adjective positions
Describe things

1 Grammar chart: adjective position

Note:
- Adjectives come before the noun in English, e.g. *This is an interesting book*. NOT ~~*This is a book interesting*~~.
- Adjectives can also come after some verbs, e.g. *be, feel, appear* e.g. *This car is fast.*

See Grammar summary page 106.

2 Controlled practice of adjective order

- Read the jumbled sentences.
- Put the words in the correct order.
- Remember to put adjectives in the right order.

Answers
1 This is a light surfboard.
2 My brother likes fast cars.
3 Do you want a big TV?
4 Where is my new MP3 player?
5 I want a cheap bike for school.
6 I can't use this old computer.

3 Controlled practice; transformation of sentences with adjectives

- Look at the picture.
- Rewrite the sentences using *be* and the adjectives.

Answers
1 Her hair is short and blond
2 are blue
3 is new and beautiful
4 is fast
5 is big
6 is expensive
7 are cool

Finished?
- Fast finishers can do Puzzle 6B on page 96.

Answers
Ronaldo's

Over to you!

4 Oral practice of describing things

- Think of an electronic gadget.
- Take turns to use the skeleton description to describe the gadget.
- Use appropriate adjectives.
- Other students try to guess the object.

➡ **Workbook page 27**
➡ **Mixed Ability Worksheets page 13**

Living English

Aims

Read an article about robots in films and TV programs
Identify the correct statements about a reading text
Match descriptions to photos
Choose the correct information from statements about a listening text
Understand the position of adjective.
Write about favorite gadgets using appropriate adjectives and adjective position

Reading

 **Class CD1 track 49**

Cultural note

- **Robocop** is a 1987 science fiction movie. Peter Weller (who also appears in the fifth series of *24*, with Kiefer Sutherland) plays a cyborg policeman. There were two sequels to the film and also a TV series.
- **The Terminator** is a 1984 science fiction movie. Arnold Schwarzenegger plays a deadly cyborg, a half-human, half-robot. There were two sequels to The Terminator movie – *Terminator 2: Judgement Day* and *Terminator 3: Rise of the Machines.*
- **I, Robot** is a 2004 science fiction film. Will Smith plays a policeman investigating a murder. In his work he discovers that a group of robots are trying to take over the world. He is helped by a robot called Sonny.
- **Dr Who** is a British TV series. The Dr is a time traveller, who has adventures in different periods of the past and the future.
- **Lost in Space** was an American television series from the 1960s. It was about the adventures of the Robinson family in 1997 who were exploring space. The film from the TV series was made in 1998 and starred Matt LeBlanc from the popular TV comedy *Friends*.

Warm-up

Books closed. What famous robots do students know? Where did they appear? What are their names? Are they good or bad robots? What do they do? Open books. Look at the photos. Do they know any of the robots (see Cultural note).

1 Global comprehension task (first reading)

- Read the question.
- Read the article quickly.
- Choose the correct answer.

Answers

2 robots from movies and TV shows

2 Detailed comprehension task (second reading)

- Read the statements.
- Read the article again.
- Write the names of the robots next to the statements.

Answers

1 Robot
2 Detective Spooner
3 K9
4 Robocop
5 Terminator

Extra activity (stronger classes)

Personalization; adjective practice; *can* for ability

Personalization activities give students the opportunity to express themselves in many areas of language.

- Ask students which robot they like the best from exercise 1.
- In pairs, students design their own robot.
- Encourage them to describe their robot using adjectives and its abilities.
- Students can cut out pictures from magazines to make their robot or draw them themselves.
- Pin the descriptions on the wall and encourage students to read about their classmates' robots.
- Vote on the nicest / most intelligent / best robot.

Listening

1 Global comprehension of listening text (first listening)

- Look at the photos and the names of the robots.
- Listen to the descriptions.
- Write the name of the robots under the correct photos.

Audio CD 1 track 50

This robot is called Robbie. He's a good robot and helps people. He's the first robot to be in a movie. His head has lights and they flash. He has a big body with control buttons. He can walk and turn. He has big feet and short arms. He doesn't look human. He's a robot from 1956.

This robot is called C-3PO. He's a smart robot and he's in the *Star Wars* movies. He's a good friend to R2-D2. He's tall, he's metal and golden, and he has a head and body like a human. He can do amazing things for example he can speak a million languages.

Answers

C-3PO is on the left.
Robbie is on the right.

2 Detailed comprehension of listening text (second listening)

- Read the statements.
- Listen again.
- Circle the correct information.

Audio CD 1 track 50

Answers

Robbie
1 robot
2 good
3 big
4 short
5 old

C-3PO
1 tall
2 hard
3 smart
4 R2-D2
5 many languages

Writing

1 Model writing text

- Read the text.

2 Word order of adjectives

- Read the Writing skills box.

Writing Skills: Word order: position of adjectives

- Adjectives go before nouns, e.g. *This is an interesting gadget.*
- Adjectives can also go after verbs like *be, feel* and *appear*, e.g. *This gadget is interesting.*
- When adjectives come directly after a verb, it emphasises the adjective in a sentence.

3 Practice of word order of adjectives

- Read the sentences.
- Check (✓) the correct sentences.

Answers

1 ✗ 2 ✗ 3 ✓ 4 ✓

4 Detailed comprehension of model writing text

- Read the chart.
- Read the information about Carl's favorite electronic gadgets in exercise 1 again.
- Fill in the chart

Answers

Description	Uses
1 big, heavy	use the Internet; chat with friends
2 small, big screen	send text messages

5 Preparation for personalized writing

- Think about your favorite gadgets.
- Fill in the chart with the description and uses of your favorite gadgets.

6 Personalized writing

- Follow the model writing text.
- Use your own ideas from the chart to change the text.
- Write a description of your favorite gadgets.

➡ **Tests page 12**

3 Review

Vocabulary

1
1 water, soda
2 coffee
3 ketchup, oil, soda, water
4 apple, bananas, bread, cheese, French fries, sausages
5 salt

2
1 hair
2 ear
3 mouth
4 neck
5 arm
6 leg
7 eye
8 nose
9 hand
10 knee
11 feet

3
1 heavy
2 slow
3 old
4 hard
5 small
6 expensive

Grammar

1
1 a
2 some
3 a
4 some
5 any
6 a

2
1 are some
2 isn't any
3 is a
4 There is some
5 There aren't any

3
1 any
2 any
3 Is there any
4 Are there any
5 Is there an

4
1 Whose backpack is this?
It's mine.
2 Whose tennis racket is this?
It's hers.
3 Who book is this?
It's yours.
4 Whose guitar is this?
It's his.
5 Whose soccer ball is this?
It's theirs.
6 Whose school flag is this?
It's ours.

5
1 is small
2 has a small
3 is black and white
4 has a black and white
5 have a big
6 is big
7 is electric
8 has an electric

6 Students' own answers

7 Consumer world

Unit summary

Active vocabulary
- noun categories: baggage, food, furniture, money, music, time, traffic, travel
- groceries: apples, chicken, ice cream, juice, muffins, paper towels, rice, soap, toothpaste, yogurt

Passive vocabulary
- nouns: armchair, arrangements, backpack, cake, cleaning products, comfortable, downtown, essentials, habit, healthy, hour, information, item, label, lifetime, luck, (special) offer, packet, phone card, quote, refrigerator, sugar, teaspoon, thought, variety, nutrition
- verbs: kill, fish, spill, window shop
- adjectives: wet

Grammar
- *How much / How many* + quantifiers
- *Would you like … ?*

Skills
- Reading unusual and interesting information about food and drink
- Writing a profile of your buying habits; writing in paragraphs
- Making and responding to requests using *Would you like … ?*

Cross-curricular
- science

Values
- consumer education, health

Exploring the topic

Vocabulary

Aims
Present noun categories
Model *How much / How many* + quantifiers

Warm-up
Do students watch advertisements on TV or read them in magazines? Do they think advertisements work? What are their favourite advertisements? Why?

1 Presentation of vocabulary set: noun categories

- Read the words in 1–8.
- Write the words in box next to the correct words 1–8.
- Listen, check and repeat.

Answers / Audio CD 2 track 2

1 songs, music
2 bags, baggage
3 dollars, money
4 hours, time
5 trips, travel
6 cars, traffic
7 meals, food
8 chairs and tables, furniture

2 Vocabulary practice; exposure to *How much / How many* + quantifiers

- Read the sentences.
- Read the advertisements.
- Fill in the sentences with the correct nouns / noun categories from exercise 1.
- Listen and check.

Audio CD 2 track 3

Answers

1 meals
2 baggage
3 traffic, hours
4 money
5 furniture
6 trip

Extra activity (stronger classes)

Further practice of vocabulary; personalization

Students write their own consumer comments.
- Tell students to look at the advertisements again.
- Students write their own consumer comments.
- Stick a copy of each advertisement on the wall and ask students to put their consumer comments below the advertisement.
- Students read the comments and vote on the best.

Extend your vocabulary (Workbook page 28)
Things in a city: billboard department store road signs skyscraper sidewalk stop light

➡ **Workbook page 28**

Grammar

> ***Aims***
> Present and practice *How much / How many* + quantifiers
> Review *There is / There are*
> Ask about quantities of things

1 Grammar chart: *How much / How many* + quantifiers

Note:
We use *How much / How many* to ask about the quantity of things. We use:
- *How many* with countable nouns, e.g. *How many people are there?*
- *How much* with uncountable nouns, e.g. *How much cheese is there?*

We use *There is / are none* or *There isn't / aren't any* to indicate a zero quantity. We use:
- a plural verb form with countable nouns: *There are none* or *There aren't any*.
- a singular verb form with uncountable nouns: *There is none* or *There isn't any*.

We use *a few / a little* and *not many / not much* to indicate a small quantity. We use:
- *There are a few* and *There aren't many* with countable plural nouns, e.g. *There are a few chairs. There aren't many songs.*
- *There is a little* and *There isn't much* with uncountable nouns, e.g. *There is a little furniture. There isn't much music.*

We use *a lot of* to indicate a large quantity. We use:
- *There are a lot of* with countable plural nouns, e.g. *There are a lot of bags.*
- *There is a lot of* with uncountable nouns, e.g. *There is a lot of baggage.*

See Grammar summary page 106.

2 Controlled practice of countable / uncountable nouns; review of category nouns

- Look at the words in the chart in exercise 1.
- Write C (countable) or U (uncountable) next to each word.

Answers

1 U	5 C	9 C	13 C
2 C	6 U	10 U	14 U
3 C	7 U	11 U	15 U
4 C	8 C	12 C	

3 Controlled practice of quantifiers + countable / uncountable nouns; review of category nouns

- Read the sentences and look at the quantifiers before the nouns.
- Circle the correct noun.

Answers

1 furniture	3 cars	5 songs
2 hours	4 food	

4 Controlled practice of *How much / How many* + countable / uncountable nouns

- Read the questions and look at the nouns.
- Fill in the questions with *How much* or *How many*.

Answers

1 How much	4 How much
2 How many	5 How many
3 How much	

5 Controlled practice of quantifiers

- Read the questions in exercise 4 again.
- Look at the picture of Future City.
- Fill in the answers to the questions in exercise 4 with *a little*, *a few*, or *a lot of*.

Answers

1 a little	4 a lot of
2 a few	5 a few
3 a little	

Finished?

Fast finishers can do Puzzle 7A on page 98.

Answers

TIME IS MONEY
TRAVEL LIGHT

Over to you!

6 Personalization; written / oral practice of *There is / There are* + quantifiers

- Write sentences to describe your bedroom, using *There is / isn't, There are / aren't + any, few / little, many / much* + noun.
- Exchange your sentences with another student.
- Take turns to tell the class about another student's bedroom.

➡ **Workbook page 29**
➡ **Mixed Ability Worksheets page 14**

Building the topic

Vocabulary

Aims

Present and practice groceries vocabulary
Model *Would you like …?* for offers and requests
Model responses to offers and requests
Review countable and uncountable nouns

Warm-up

Books closed. Write the letters a–z on the board. In pairs, students try to write one item of food / drink beginning with each letter. Give students two minutes to write as many words as possible. Which pair has the longest list?

1 Presentation of vocabulary set: groceries

- Look at the poster.
- Fill in the blanks in the advertisement with the correct words in the box.
- Listen, check and repeat.

Answers / Audio CD 2 track 4

1 paper towels	6 apples
2 soap	7 yogurt
3 toothpaste	8 juice
4 muffins	9 chicken
5 rice	10 ice cream

2 Vocabulary practice; exposure to *Would you like …?* and responses to requests

- Read the dialog between Roy and Nelson.
- Complete Nelson's shopping list.
- Listen and check.

Audio CD 2 track 5

Answers

Food: chicken, ice cream, yogurt, two red apples, muffins
Drinks: orange juice
Household products: toothpaste, paper towels

3 Vocabulary practice; review of countable / uncountable nouns

- Look at the shopping list in exercise 2 again.
- Put the words in the correct column: countable / uncountable.

Answers

Countable: phone card, apples, muffins, paper towels
Uncountable: rice, chicken, ice cream, yoghurt, orange juice, soap, toothpaste

Extend your vocabulary (Workbook page 30)

Groceries: grapes potatoes shampoo steak tomatoes toothbrush

➡ **Workbook page 30**

Grammar

Aims

Present and practice *Would you like …?* and appropriate responses
Make offers and requests

1 Grammar chart: *Would you like …?*

Note:

- We use *Would you like …?* to make requests.
- We use *some* with plural countable nouns and uncountable nouns in questions with *Would you like …?*, e.g. *Would you like some muffins / yogurt?*
- The affirmative form is *I / you / he / she / we / they* + *would like*. We often contract *would* to *'d*.

See Grammar summary page 107.

2 Controlled practice of making requests with *I'd like.*

- Read the words in the box.
- Look at the stores in pictures 1–6.
- Write requests for each store using *I'd like* and an appropriate phrase in the box.

Answers

1 I'd like a new cell phone.
2 I'd like a good hip hop CD.
3 I'd like some money.
4 I'd like a comfortable armchair.
5 I'd like a cool backpack.
6 I'd like a fast bike.

3 Controlled practice of making offers with *Would you like …?*

- Read the words in the box.
- Read the situations.
- Write an appropriate offer for each situations using *Would you like …?* and the words in the box.

Answers

1 Would you like a hamburger?
2 Would you like some juice?
3 Would you like a jacket?
4 Would you like a towel?
5 Would you like an umbrella?

4 Practice of responses to offers

- Read the offers.
- Look at the pictures or words next to the answers.
- Write Nelson's answers, using *That'd be great, thanks.* 👍, *Yes, please.* (👌), or *No, thanks.*👎.

Answers

1 That'd be great, thanks.
2 Yes, please.
3 That'd be great, thanks.
4 No, thanks.
5 No, thanks.
6 Yes, please.

Finished?

Fast finishers can do Puzzle 7B on page 98.

Answers

Toothpaste

Over to you!

5 Personalization; oral practice of *Would you like …?* and appropriate responses

- Think of five things to buy students in your class as a birthday present.
- With another student, take turns to ask and answer, using *Would you like …?*
- Respond appropriately.

➡ **Workbook page 31**
➡ **Mixed Ability Worksheets page 15**

Living English

Aims

Read about interesting food and drink facts
Identify the correct information in statements about a reading text
Understand the purpose of paragraphs
Identify specific information in texts
Write a profile about the places you shop, the things you buy and when you shop
Make and respond to requests using the appropriate pronunciation of *Would you …?*

Reading

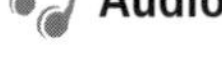 **Audio CD 2 track 6**

Warm-up

- Books closed. Write these questions on the board.
  1. *How many teaspoons of sugar does an average North American eat every day?*
  2. *How many different varieties of rice are there in the world?*
  3. *What percentage of milk is water?*
  4. *What do you do when you spill salt?*
- Discuss the questions with students and write down their answers.

1 Global comprehension task (first reading)

- Read the article quickly.
- Choose the best statement to answer the question.
- Check the answers to the questions in the warm-up.

Answers

2 Funny information about food ingredients and habits

2 Detailed comprehension task (second reading)

- Read the sentences.
- Read the article again.
- Decide if the sentences are true or false and circle *T* or *F*.

Answers

1 T 2 F 3 F 4 F 5 F 6 T

Extra activity (all classes)

Review quantifiers and simple present (negative)

Correcting false sentences provides further practice of grammar.

- Ask students to correct the false sentences in exercise 2.

Answers

2 Coffee isn't healthy.
3 Tomatoes aren't vegetables. They're fruit.
4 There are lots of varieties of rice.
5 People who read information on food packets eat less.

Writing

1 Use of paragraphs in writing

- Read the Writing skills box.

Writing skills: Using paragraphs
Paragraphs help students to:
- organize their writing;
- keep important sentences together;
- make their writing easier to read and more natural.

2 Practice identifying the subjects of paragraphs

- Read the headings.
- Read the text.
- Write the headings next to the correct paragraphs.

Answers

1 Where I shop
2 What things I buy
3 When I go shopping

3 Detailed analysis of model writing text

- Read the chart.
- Read the text again.
- Fill in the column labeled "Carolyn".

Answers

	Carolyn
Places I shop	Supermarket, small shops near her house, the Internet
Things I buy	a lot of fruit and vegetables, bread and muffins, CDs and books
When I go shopping	To the supermarket once a month, window shopping on Saturdays

4 Preparation for personalized writing

- Think about your shopping habits.
- Fill in the column labeled "You" with your own information.

5 Personalized writing

- Follow the model writing text.
- Use your own information from the chart in exercise 4.
- Write a text about your consumer profile.

Speaking

1 First listening

- Look at the pictures and read the model dialogs quickly.
- Listen and read.

Audio CD 2 track 7

2 Presentation of pronunciation point

Pronunciation: *Would you …?*
Would you is often pronounced as one word in conversation, as /wʊdʒu/.

- Read the examples in the Pronunciation box.
- Listen to the examples and repeat, copying the pronunciation of *Would you*.

Audio CD 2 track 8

3 Pronunciation practice

- Read the offers.
- Practice saying the sentences, pronouncing *Would* you as /wʊdʒu/.
- Listen and repeat.

Audio CD 2 track 9

4 Dialog practice

- Practice the model dialogs with another student.
- Change roles and practice again.

5 Dialog personalization and practice

- Look at the words in blue in the model dialog.
- Think of some different foods and responses.
- Replace the blue words with your ideas to make a new dialog.
- Practice the dialog with another student.

➡ **Tests page 14**

8 One of a kind

Unit summary

Active vocabulary

- jobs: artist, guitarist, leader, runner, fashion designer, inventor, politician, songwriter
- feelings: bored, happy, nervous, sad, scared, surprised, tired

Passive vocabulary

- nouns: accident, airplane, astronaut, flight, human rights, jockey, lap, medal, Moon, performance, pilot, race, shuttle, space, track
- adjectives: amazing, similar, successful, talented

Grammar

- *was / were*
- ordinal numbers

Skills

- Reading about famous people and their achievements; identifying the content of a paragraph using headings
- Listening to a profile of a famous person
- Talking about where and when you were born; pronunciation of /θ/ in ordinal numbers

Cross-curricular

- sport, music, history

Values

- multicultural societies

Exploring the topic

Vocabulary

Aims
Present and practice jobs
Model *was / were*

Warm-up

Look at the photos. Do students recognize any of the people? Do they know what they did? Would students like to do these jobs?

Cultural note

- **Martin Luther King** (1929–1968) was a minister and leader of the American civil rights movement.
- **Florence Griffith-Joyner** (1959–1998) was an American athlete who holds the World Record for running the 100m and 200m.
- **Newman Darby** (1924–) designed and built boats.
- **Frida Kahlo** (1907–1954) was a Mexican painter.
- **Jimi Hendrix** (1942–1970) was an American musician, singer and songwriter.

1 Presentation of vocabulary set: jobs

- Look at texts A–E.
- Write the letter of the text next to the jobs. You can use the numbers more than once.
- Listen, check and repeat.

Answers / Audio CD 2 track 10

A fashion designer, runner
B artist
C leader, politician
D inventor
E guitarist, songwriter

2 Vocabulary practice; exposure to *was / were*

- Read and listen to the text.
- Write the number of the photos next to each paragraph.

Audio CD 2 track 11

Answers
A 2 B 4 C 1 D 3 E 5

3 Exposure to *was / were*; text comprehension

- Read the sentences.
- Read the text again.
- Write the number of the correct paragraph next to each sentence.

Answers
1 B 2 D 3 A 4 B 5 E 6 D

Extend your vocabulary (Workbook page 32)
Jobs: author, composer, explorer, movie director, queen, racing driver

➡ **Workbook page 32**

Grammar

Aims

Present and practice *was / were* (affirmative, negative, questions and short answers)
Talk about the past

Cultural note

- **Pelé** (born October 23, 1940) is a former Brazilian footballer. In his career, Pelé won three World Cups with Brazil and holds a record of scoring 1281 goals in 1363 matches.
- **Muhammad Ali** (born January 17, 1942 as Cassius Marcellus Clay) is a former American heavyweight boxer. His nickname was "The Greatest" and in his career he won 56 out of his 61 fights.

1 Grammar chart: *was / were* (affirmative and negative)

Note:
- The affirmative past form of *be* is *was / were*.
- The negative past form of *be* is *wasn't (= was not) / weren't (= were not).*

See Grammar summary page 107.

2 Controlled practice of *was / were* (affirmative and negative)

- Look at the timeline about Pelé.
- Fill in the sentences with the correct affirmative or negative form of *be*.

Answers

1	wasn't	4	weren't
2	were	5	was
3	was	6	wasn't

3 Grammar chart: *was / were* (questions and short answers)

Note:
- We make questions with *be* in the past by swapping the verb and the subject.

See Grammar summary page 107.

4 Controlled practice of *was / were* (*yes / no* questions and short answers)

- Look at the timeline about Muhammad Ali.
- Read the skeleton questions.
- Write questions using *was / were*.
- Use the information in the timeline to write short answers.

Answers

1 Was he in the USA in 1942? Yes, he was.
2 Was he born in Brazil? No, he wasn't.
3 Was he Olympic Champion in 1960? Yes, he was.
4 Was he World Champion in 1962? No, he wasn't.

Extra activity (all classes)

Further practice of *was / were*

Students play a guessing game about true / false facts about other students.

- Students write five sentences – three true and two false – using *was / were*, e.g. *I was born in 1994. My grandfather was an actor.*
- In pairs, students swap their sentences and guess which are the false sentences.

Finished?

Fast finishers can do Puzzle 8A on page 98.

Answers

Gianni Versace was an Italian fashion designer.

Over to you!

5 Oral practice of *was / were* (affirmative, negative, questions and short answers)

- Look through the unit and choose a famous person.
- Make some notes if necessary.
- Take turns to describe the person and guess who it is.

➡ **Workbook page 33**
➡ **Mixed Ability Worksheets page 16**

Building the topic

Vocabulary

Aims

Present and practice feelings
Model ordinal numbers
Review *was / were* (affirmative)

Cultural note

- **The Tower of London** is a building in central London which in its history has been used as a royal palace, a private zoo and a prison. It was built in 1078 and is now a tourist attraction and home of the Crown Jewels – a collection of crowns and other British royal jewelry.

Warm-up

What are students' favorite memories of the past? Where were they? Who were they with? Why are they favorite memories? How do students record their memories? Do they take photos or keep a diary?

1 Vocabulary presentation; exposure to *was / were*

- Read the words in the box.
- Read the text again and find the adjectives in the box and underline them.
- Write the meanings of the adjectives in your own language.
- Listen and repeat.

Answers / Audio CD 2 track 12

A nervous
B surprised
C happy
D bored
E sad
F tired
G scared

2 Text comprehension

- Read the statements.
- Read the descriptions again.
- Write the names of the people next to the correct statement.

Audio CD 2 track 13

Answers

1 Delia
2 Evan
3 Eduardo
4 Damon
5 Michaela
6 Gillian
7 Casper

Extra activity (all classes)

Review of adjectives

Students review adjectives in a simple game.

- Draw a picture of your (imaginary) pet on the board.
- Write *I love my cat / dog /* etc *because he's / she's …*
- Write the letters a–z down the board.
- Ask students to call out appropriate adjectives beginning with each letter, e.g. *amazing*, *beautiful*, etc.

Extend your vocabulary (Workbook page 34)
Feelings: disappointed excited jealous sick worried

➡ **Workbook page 34**

Grammar

Aims
Present and practice ordinal numbers
Review *be* (simple present and simple past)

1 Grammar chart: ordinal numbers

Note:
- We use ordinal numbers to talk about the order of things.
- Many ordinal numbers are made by adding *-th* to the normal number, e.g. *four* ➡ *fourth*.
- Exceptions include *one* ➡ *first*, *two* ➡ *second*, *three* ➡ *third*, *five* ➡ *fifth*, *twelve* ➡ *twelfth*.
- We also use ordinal numbers in dates, e.g. *June fifth* NOT ~~*June five*~~.

See Grammar summary page 107.

Take note!
last
- The last thing, event, or person is the one that comes after all the others, e.g. *I missed the last bus.*

2 Controlled practice of writing ordinal numbers
- Read the numbers.
- Write the ordinal number in words.

Answers
1 twenty-fifth
2 eighty-ninth
3 seventy-sixth
4 sixty-third
5 ninetieth

3 Controlled practice of cardinal / ordinal numbers
- Read the sentences.
- Circle the correct form of the number.

Answers
1 twentieth
2 second
3 thirty-two
4 third
5 twelfth

4 Controlled practice of ordinal numbers
- Look at the picture.
- Read the sentences and find the students in the picture.
- Fill in the sentences with the correct ordinal number.

Answers
1 eighth, ninth
2 third
3 fourteenth / last
4 seventh
5 twelfth and thirteenth
6 first

Finished?
Fast finishers can do Puzzle 8B on page 98.

Answers
1 tired
2 bored
3 surprised
4 scared

Over to you!

5 Class dynamics; personalization; oral practice of sports and ordinal numbers
- Read the sports in the box.
- Guess the order of the sports from the most popular (first) to the least popular (last) for your class.
- Take turns to read your list to the class (see example).
- Give your opinion of other students' orders.

Extra activity (all classes)

Further practice of ordinal numbers in dates
Students match dates and events and practice numbers in dates.
- Write some famous dates from the history of the world or your students' country on the board, e.g. *July 20, 1969*. (The first moon landings).
- Ask students if they know what happened on that day but do not say whether they are right / wrong.
- Write the events on the board.
- Students match the dates and the events.
- In feedback, check students are using ordinals in dates correctly.

➡ Workbook page 35
➡ Mixed Ability Worksheets page 17

Living English

Aims

Read an article about famous people and their achievements
Use headings to identify the main content of sections in a reading text
Listen to a profile of a famous person
Identify specific information from a listening text
Talk about where and when you were born
Pronounce /θ/ sounds in ordinal numbers

Reading

Audio CD 2 track 14

Cultural note

- **Concorde** was a type of passenger plane which could travel at supersonic speeds of about 2,170 km/h. Its first commercial flight was in 1976.
- **Amelia Earhart** (1897–1937) was the first woman to fly solo across the Atlantic Ocean. She disappeared in 1937 while trying to fly around the world. The American government spent $4 million looking for Earhart but never found her or her plane.
- **The first moon landing** was on July 20, 1969. There have been six moon landings and twelve astronauts have walked on the moon.
- **The Triple Crown** is a series of three horse races, in Kentucky, Maryland and New York in America. In over 125 years, only eleven horses have ever won all three races.
- **The Indianapolis 500** is a 500-mile car race which is held every year in Indiana, America. The event started in 1911.

Warm-up

- Books closed. Do students know the names of any of the following people?
  1 The first person on the moon (Neil Armstrong).
  2 The first president of their country.
  3 The first president of the United States (George Washington).
  4 The first person in the classroom today.
  5 The person who usually leaves the classroom last.

1 Pre-reading task

- Look at the title of the text and the photos.
- Who do students recognize? Why were they famous?

Answers

See text and Cultural note.

2 Presentation and practice of reading skill (first reading)

- Read the Reading skills box.

Reading skills: Using headings

- Headings are often brief summaries of the content of paragraphs. Reading a heading before reading a text will help you understand the overall meaning of a paragraph.

- Read the headings.
- Read the questions.
- Decide which section tells you the answers to the questions. How did you decide?
- Read the article.
- Write the answers to the questions.

Answers

1 Section 2: Eugene Cernan
2 Section 3: In 2005
3 Section 1: In July, 1937

3 Detailed comprehension task (second reading)

- Read the questions.
- Read the article again.
- Write the answers.

Answers

1 Jackie Robinson
2 Twelve seconds
3 Uri Gagarin
4 On October 24th, 2003
5 Julie Krone
6 In December, 1972

Listening

Cultural note

- **Andre Agassi** (born April 29, 1970) was an American tennis player until he retired in 2006. He has won eight Grand Slam titles, including the US Open and Wimbledon. He is married to the former women's number one tennis player, Steffi Graf.

1 Comprehension of listening text (first listening)

- Look at the photos and listen.
- Answer the questions.

Answers / Audio CD 2 track 15

André Agassi is a great tennis player. He was born in 1970 in Las Vegas, USA. In 1974 he had a game of tennis with the great tennis player Jimmy Connors. He was only four years old! His first important match against Pete Sampras was in 1980 at a junior tournament. In 1986, he was in a professional match for the first time, but he wasn't the winner. In 1987, he was the winner of his first Grand prix title, in Brazil. He wasn't always a great player – in 1989, he was only the seventh in the world of tennis. But in 1992, he was the winner at Wimbledon, and in 1994, he was the number two player in the world. From 1997 to 1999, he was married to Brooke Shields, the famous actress, but he was not very successful during those years. He's still famous in the world of sports today.

2 Detailed comprehension of listening text (second listening)

- Read the sentences.
- Listen to the profile again.
- Circle the correct years in the sentences.

Answers

1 1974
2 1980
3 1987
4 1989
5 1994
6 1999

Speaking

1 First listening

- Look at the pictures and read the model dialog quickly.
- Listen and read.

Audio CD 2 track 16

2 Presentation of pronunciation point

Pronunciation: /θ/ sound
When ordinal numbers end in *-th*, these letters are pronounced as /θ/.

- Read the examples in the Pronunciation box.
- Listen to the examples and repeat, copying the sound /θ/ at the end of the ordinal numbers.

Audio CD 2 track 17

3 Pronunciation practice

- Read the numbers.
- Listen and circle the number you hear.
- Listen and repeat / check.

Answers / Audio CD 2 track 18

1 twelfth
2 sixty-six
3 twenty
4 fourth
5 hundredth

4 Dialog practice

- Practice the model dialogs with another student.
- Change roles and practice again.

5 Dialog personalization and practice

- Look at the words in blue in the model dialog.
- Think of a different dates and ages.
- Replace the blue words with your ideas to make a new dialog.
- Practice the dialog with another student.

➡ **Tests page 16**

4 Review

Vocabulary

1
1 H
2 B
3 G
4 A
5 F
6 D
7 C
8 E

2
soap ✓
toothpaste ✗
paper towels ✓
rice ✗
muffins ✗
apples ✓
yogurt ✓
juice ✓
chicken ✓
ice cream ✗

3
1 inventor
2 artist
3 fashion designer
4 guitarist
5 politician
6 leader
7 songwriter
8 runner

4
1 nervous
2 tired
3 bored
4 scared
5 sad
6 surprised

Grammar

1
1 There is a lot of furniture.
2 There are a few tables.
3 There is a little baggage.
4 There isn't any coffee.
5 There isn't much food.
6 There aren't many people.

2
1 **A:** Would you like
B: 'd like
2 **B:** we'd like
3 **A:** Would you like
4 **A:** Would you and your friends like
5 **A:** Would you like
B: that would be

3
1 were
2 was
3 was
4 Were
5 weren't
6 were
7 was
8 wasn't

4
1 twenty-seventh
2 twentieth
3 twenty-fourth
4 seventeenth
5 third
6 thirtieth

Study skills

Students' own answers

9 Life changes

Unit summary

Active vocabulary
- transport: by boat, by car, by plane, by ship, by train, on foot
- irregular verbs: build, give, meet, run, see, spend, tell, go
- other: argue, crash, miss, try

Passive vocabulary
- nouns: Argentina, bat, beach, charity, Cuba, Dominican Republic, equipment, Germany, glove, hill, home run, Italy, milk carton, mountain, ocean, police officer, Sumatra, superstar, tape, tree, Ukraine, wave
- verbs: arrest, clean, destroy, forget, melt, move
- adjectives: Chinese, Cuban, dead, German, Italian, married, Ukrainian

Grammar
- simple past regular verbs (affirmative)
- simple past irregular verbs (affirmative)

Skills
- Reading a profile of a sportsman
- Writing a description of a vacation
- Talking about what you did during the summer; pronouncing regular past tense endings

Cross-curricular
- geography, science, history, sport

Values
- multicultural societies, environment

Exploring the topic

Vocabulary

Aims
Present and practice forms of transport and ways of traveling
Model simple past regular and irregular verbs (affirmative)

Warm-up

Do students know their family history? Were their parents / grandparents born in the country they live in now? If not, where did they come from? Why did they move? Do students know any famous immigrants in their countries? Where did they come from?

1 Presentation of vocabulary set: transport

- Look at the photos.
- Read the phrases in the box.
- Write the number of the photos next to the correct phrases.

Answers / Audio CD 2 track 19

1 by ship	4 by boat
2 by train	5 by plane
3 on foot	6 by car

2 Exposure to simple past regular verbs (affirmative)

- Read the list of verbs.
- Read the text.
- Find the past forms of the verbs in the text.
- Write the past forms next to each verb.

Answers / Audio CD 2 track 20

Answers

1 moved	5 started
2 traveled	6 carried
3 stopped	7 arrived
4 stayed	8 learned

3 Text comprehension; practice of simple present and simple past of *be*

- Read the statements.
- Read the text again.
- Write the correct name next to each statement.

Answers

1 Christine	4 David
2 Ruey	5 Alicia
3 Katia	6 Esteban

Extend your vocabulary (Workbook page 36)
Transport: helicopter kayak subway train truck van yacht

➡ **Workbook page 36**

Grammar

Aims

Present and practice simple past regular verbs (affirmative)
Present and practice spelling rules for simple past regular verbs
Present and practice past time expressions
Talk about actions in the past

1 Grammar chart: simple past regular verbs (affirmative)

Note:

- We use the simple past to talk about actions that started and finished in the past.
- We make the simple past of regular verbs by adding *-ed* to the verb.
- The simple past form of verbs is the same for all persons, e.g. *I / you* (singular) */ he / she / it / you* (plural) */ they walked.*
- For spelling rules of simple past regular forms, see *Take note!* (below).

See Grammar summary page 107.

Take note!

Spelling rules

We make the simple past of regular verbs:

- by adding *-ed*, e.g. *learn* ➡ *learned*, *play* ➡ *played*
- ending in *-e* by adding *-d*, e.g. *move* ➡ *moved*
- ending in a consonant and *y* by changing the *y* to *i* and adding *-ed*, e.g. *carry* ➡ *carried*
- ending in one vowel + one consonant by doubling the final consonant and adding *-ed*, e.g. *stop* ➡ *stopped.* Common exceptions to this rule are words ending in *-l*, e.g. *travel* ➡ *traveled.*

2 Controlled practice of simple past regular verbs (affirmative)

- Read the sentences.
- Fill in the sentences with the simple past affirmative of the verbs in parentheses.

Answers

1 traveled	4 played
2 studied	5 stopped
3 arrived	

3 Controlled practice of simple past regular verbs (affirmative)

- Read the verbs in the box.
- Look at the pictures.
- Fill in the sentences with the simple past affirmative of the correct verb in the box.

Answers

1 dropped	4 tried
2 missed	5 crashed
3 arrived	6 argued

Take note!

Past time expressions

We use certain past time expressions to talk about when actions in the past happened. We use:

- *in* + year, e.g. *We moved to Paris in 1995.*
- *x years / months / weeks / days / hours / minutes + ago*, e.g. *My grandparents moved to Germany fifty years ago.*
- *yesterday*, e.g. *They arrived yesterday.*
- *last + week / month / year*, e.g. *I traveled to England last year.*

4 Free practice of past time expressions

- Read the phrases.
- Write true sentences about your past using the simple past affirmative and an appropriate time expression.

Possible answers

1 I started school seven years ago.
2 I learned to swim in 2001.
3 I traveled by car yesterday.
4 I missed a bus last week.
5 I argued with my best friend last month.

Finished?

Fast finishers can do Puzzle 9A on page 99.

Answers

train (from Tina Ryan)

Over to you!

5 Personalization; written and oral practice of simple past regular verbs (affirmative)

- Write some true or false sentences about your past.
- Take turns to tell the class (see example).
- Are students' statements true or false?

➡ **Workbook page 37**
➡ **Mixed Ability Worksheets page 18**

Building the topic

Vocabulary

Aims

Present and practice simple past irregular verbs
Review simple past regular (affirmative)
Model simple past irregular (affirmative)

Cultural note

- A **tsunami** is a wave or series of waves that is caused by earthquakes and volcanic eruptions. An earthquake in the Indian Ocean in 2004 caused a series of tsunamis which hit several countries including Indonesia, Thailand, Malaysia, India and Sri Lanka. Over 230,000 people died.

Warm-up

Do students remember the tsunami in 2004? Where were they when they heard about the disaster? What other disasters like this do they know about?

1 Presentation of vocabulary set: irregular verbs (simple past forms)

- Read the list of verbs.
- Read the simple past forms of the verbs in the box.
- Write the correct simple past forms next to the verbs.
- Listen and check / repeat.

Answers / Audio CD 2 track 21

1 tell, told	5 run, ran
2 give, gave	6 go, went
3 see, saw	7 spend, spent
4 meet, met	8 build, built

2 Exposure to simple past irregular verbs; text comprehension

- Look at the pictures.
- Read and listen to the story.
- Number the pictures in the order of the story.

Audio CD 2 track 22

Answers

4 2 3
5 8 7
6 1

3 Practice of vocabulary set; further text comprehension

- Read the sentences.
- Read the story again.
- Write T (True) or F (False) next to each statement.
- Correct the false statements.

Answers

1 F – Adi saw the wave first.
2 F – Adi and his family climbed a hill.
3 T
4 F – Some people at the top of the hill gave his family water and food.
5 T
6 T

Extend your vocabulary (Workbook page 38)
Irregular verbs: came did got up rode sent

➡ **Workbook page 38**

Grammar

Aims

Present and practice simple past irregular verbs (affirmative)
Present irregular verb list on page 109
Talk about actions in the past

1 Grammar chart: Simple past irregular verbs (affirmative)

Note:
- Irregular verbs have their own past forms, e.g. *run* ➡ *ran*, *go* ➡ *went*.

See Grammar summary page 108.

Take note!

Irregular verbs in simple past
- You have to learn the simple past forms of irregular verbs.

See the list on page 109.

2 Controlled practice of simple past irregular verbs (affirmative)

- Read the verbs in the box.
- Read the sentences.
- Fill in the sentences with the simple past affirmative of the correct verbs in the box.

Answers

1 saw	3 told	5 ran
2 gave	4 went	6 spent

3 Controlled practice of simple past regular and irregular verb forms

- Read the verbs.
- Write the simple past form of the verbs.
- Note that three of the verbs are regular and there is a list of irregular verb forms on page 109 of the Student's Book.

Answers

1 won	4 taught	7 returned	10 stayed
2 bought	5 built	8 met	11 went
3 married	6 gave	9 saw	

4 Controlled practice of simple past regular and irregular verbs forms in sentences

- Look at the picture and read the sentences.
- Fill in the sentences with the correct simple past form of the verbs in exercise 3.

Answers

1 won	5 returned, gave
2 bought	6 built
3 went, stayed	7 taught
4 saw	8 met, married

Finished?

Fast finishers can do Puzzle 9B on page 99.

Answers

1 TRAVELED	4 MOVED
2 MET	5 WENT
3 SAW	

The person is JAMES BOND

Over to you!

5 Personalization; written practice of simple past regular and irregular (affirmative)

- Write a sentence in the simple past about you but do not include the verb (see example).
- Exchange your sentence with another student.
- Can you complete your partner's sentence with the correct verb?

Extra activity (stronger classes)

Further practice of simple past regular and irregular verbs (affirmative)

Students practice simple past forms orally in a memory game.

- Give students, or ask them, to write a past tense verb.
- Tell students: *Yesterday I went downtown and I bought some bread.*
- The first student should say: *Yesterday I went downtown and I brought some bread* then add their own activity to the chain using the verb they chose.
- Continue until all students have spoken or no one can remember the chain.

Language note:
- We use a subject pronoun with the simple past in English, e.g. *I went to the supermarket yesterday*. NOT ~~*Went to the supermarket yesterday.*~~

➡ Workbook page 39
➡ Mixed Ability Worksheets page 19

Living English

Aims

Read a profile of a famous baseball player
Find specific information in a reading text
Describe and express your opinion about a vacation
Talk about your vacation using the correct pronunciation of simple past verbs that end in *-ed*

Reading

 **Audio CD 2 track 23**

Cultural note

- **The Dominican Republic** is a country on the eastern side of the Caribbean island of Hispaniola. Its capital is Santo Domingo and its population is about 9 million.

Warm-up

Who are students' sporting heroes? What sport they play? Why do they admire them? Are they from their country or other countries? Who are the best sportsmen and women from their countries? What do they know about them?

1 Global comprehension task (first reading)

- Read the prompts.
- Read the article quickly, looking for keywords (numbers and dates) to find the answers.
- Write the numbers and dates next to the correct prompts.

Answers

1 November 12, 1968
2 14
3 1983
4 $3,300
5 100,000

2 Detailed comprehension task (second reading)

- Read the article again.
- Complete the sentences about Sammy's life.

Answers

1 died
2 sold, shoes
3 glove, bat
4 United States
5 started, help
6 children

Writing

Cultural note

- **Mexico** is the most northern country in Latin America. Its capital is Mexico City and its population is about 103 million.

1 Presentation of model writing text

- Read David's description of his last vacation.
- Answer the questions.

Answers

He went to Mexico.
It was a great vacation.

2 Use of commas in writing

- Read the Writing skills box.

Note:
- We use commas to seperate words or phrases in a list, e.g. We played volleyball, we ate ice cream, and we danced.

3 Detailed analysis of model writing text

- Read the chart.
- Read the description again.
- Fill in the column labeled "David's vacation".

Answers

When	Last year
What country	Mexico
Forms of transport	by plane
Exact place	hotel in Cabo San Lucas
What it was like	cool
Activities	swam in the pool, went surfing in the ocean, played volleyball, ate a lot of really good food
Opinion of vacation	great

4 Preparation for personalized writing

- Think about one of your vacations.
- Fill in the column in the chart labeled "Your vacation".
- Invent some information if you can't remember.

5 Personalized writing

- Follow the model writing text.
- Use your own ideas from the chart.
- Write about your vacation.

Speaking

Cultural note

- **Hawaii** is a group of islands in the Pacific Ocean. It is the 50th state of America but is about 2,300 miles from America. Its capital is Honolulu and its population is about 1.2 million.

1 First listening

- Look at the pictures and read the model dialog quickly.
- Listen and read.

Audio CD 2 track 24

2 Presentation of pronunciation point

Pronunciation: *-ed* ending
- When verbs end in *t* or *d*, we pronounce *-ed* endings as /ɪd/.
- When verbs end in other letters, the *e* is silent and we pronounce the *-ed* ending as /d/ or /t/, e.g. stayed /steɪd/, stopped /stɑpt/.

- Read the examples in the Pronunciation box.
- Listen to the examples and repeat, copying the pronunciation of the past tense forms.

Audio CD 2 track 25

3 Pronunciation practice

- Read the verbs.
- Write a cross (✗) next to the words with a silent *e*.

Audio CD 2 track 26

Answers

2 ✗ 3 ✗ 4 ✗

4 Dialog practice

- Practice the model dialog with another student.
- Change roles and practice again.

5 Dialog personalization and practice

- Look at the words in blue in the model dialog.
- Think of some places and activities.
- Replace the blue words with your ideas to make a new dialog.
- Practice the dialog with another student.

➡ **Tests page 18**

10 Mysteries

Unit summary

Active vocabulary
- geography: beaches, deserts, jungles, islands, mountains, rivers
- disasters: break, crash, die, disappear, hit, sink

Passive vocabulary
- nouns: castle, civilization, expedition, explanation, family members, iceberg, king, legend, pneumonia, pyramid, tomb
- verbs: discover, exist
- adjectives: permanent, relaxed

Grammar
- simple past (questions and negative)

Skills
- Reading about a mystery; reading a text quickly to get a general idea of its content
- Listening to a profile of a famous piano player
- Talking about what you did yesterday; practicing intonation in *wh-* questions

Cross-curricular
- history, music, geography

Values
- environment, work

Exploring the topic

Vocabulary

Aims

Present and practice geographical features
Model simple past (questions and short answers)

Cultural note
- **The Nazca Lines** are drawings of birds, spiders, fish and other animals on the ground in the south of Peru.
- **Easter Island** is an island in the south Pacific Ocean that is part of Chile. It is famous for hundreds of large stone faces or moai statues.
- **Machu Picchu** (see Cultural note on page 32)
- **Angkor Wat** is a temple at Angkor in Cambodia, a country in south east Asia. It was a built for a king in the 12th century.
- **Gávea Rock** is in Rio in Brazil. It is 852 metres tall and in one side of the rock there is a carving of a face.

Warm-up
Do students recognize any of the places in the pictures? What do they know about them? (See Cultural note). Has anyone ever been to any of the places?

1 Presentation of vocabulary set: geographical features

- Read the words in the box.
- Read the lists of places 1–6.
- Write the correct geographical features next to the places.
- Listen, check and repeat.

Answers / Audio CD 2 track 27

1 mountains	4 islands
2 deserts	5 jungles
3 beaches	6 rivers

2 Exposure to simple past (questions and short answers); text comprehension

- Read the possible answers to the questions in the texts.
- Read the texts A-F.
- Write the number of the mystery next to the possible answers.

Audio CD 2 track 28

Answers

1 B 2 C 3 E 4 A 5 D 6 F

Extend your vocabulary (Workbook page 40)

Geographical features: cave lake rainforest volcano waterfall

➡ Workbook page 40

Grammar

Aims

Present and practice simple past (questions and short answers)
Review simple past (affirmative)

1 Grammar chart: simple past (questions)

Note:

- We form simple past (*yes / no* questions) with *Did* + subject + verb, e.g. *Did you go?* NOT ~~*Did you went?*~~
- We form *Wh-* questions in the simple past by adding the *Wh-* word to the beginning of the *yes / no* question, e.g. *Why did you go?*

See Grammar summary page 108.

2 Recognition of simple past (questions); controlled practice of simple past (short answers)

- Read the questions.
- Write short answers in the simple past.
- Check your answers below.

Answers

1 No, they didn't
2 Yes, they did.
3 Yes, they did.
4 No, they didn't.
5 Yes, they did.
6 No, they didn't.

3 Controlled practice of simple past (*yes / no* and *wh-* questions)

- Read the skeleton questions.
- Write questions in the simple past.
- Write answers to the questions.
- Check your answers below.

Answers

1 Did Brazil win the World Cup in 1970?
Yes, they did.
2 When did they make the first talking movie?
In 1927.
3 Did Ray Tomlinson send the first e-mail message?
Yes, he did.
4 Where did Marco Polo travel in the 13th century?
He traveled the Silk Road to China.
5 Did Christopher Columbus discover the Americas?
Yes, he did.
6 Did people walk on the moon in 1969?
Yes, they did.

Finished?

Fast finishers can do Puzzle 10A on page 101.

Answers

1 river
2 desert
3 island
4 jungle
5 mountain

The mystery instrument is *drums*

Over to you!

4 Personalization; written and oral practice of simple past (*yes / no* and *wh-* questions)

- Read the skeleton sentences.
- Write some questions about last weekend.
- Take turns to ask and answer.

Possible answers

Did you go out?
Where did you go?
Did you visit friends?
Who did you visit?
Did you play sports?
What sport did you play?
Did you have fun?

➡ **Workbook page 41**
➡ **Mixed Ability Worksheets page 20**

Building the topic

Vocabulary

Aims

Present and practice disaster verbs
Review simple past (affirmative)
Model simple past (negative)

Cultural note

- **The Bermuda Triangle** is an area of about 1.2 million square kilometres between Bermuda, Puerto Rico and the southern tip of Florida. The phrase was first used in the 1960s by an American journalist who was writing about various accidents that had happened in the area.
- **The Atlantic Ocean** is the second largest ocean in the world and covers approximately 20% of the earth's surface.
- **The Titanic** was a British ship built between 1909 and 1912. It was 269 metres long and weighed over 46,000 tons. The first trip was from Southampton, England to New York, America on April 10, 1912. Two days later, the Titanic hit an iceberg in the Atlantic Ocean. There were 2,223 people on this ship and only 706 survived.
- **The Great Sphinx** is a statue of a lion with the head of a Pharaoh – a king of ancient Egypt. It is near the River Nile and the capital of Egypt, Cairo.
- **Tutankhamun** was a Pharaoh of Ancient Egypt and ruled between 1334 BC and 1325 BC. The British archaeologist Howard Carter, who was employed by Lord Carnarvon, discovered Tutankhamun's tomb November 4, 1922. For many years, there were rumors of a curse on the tomb which was responsible for the early death of some of the people who had first entered the tomb.

Warm-up

Look at the title of the text: *Historical Legends*. Do students know what this phrase means? Explain that in this case legends means theories about a historical event that are not true. Do students know any other historical legends?

1 Presentation of vocabulary set: disasters

- Read the verbs in the box.
- Look at the pictures.
- Write the correct verbs next to the pictures.
- Listen, check and repeat.

Answers / Audio CD 2 track 29

1 disappear
2 crash
3 break
4 sink
5 hit
6 die

2 Vocabulary practice; exposure to simple past negative; review of simple past affirmative

- Read and listen to the texts.
- Match the texts to the pictures.

Audio CD 2 track 30

Answers

Valley of the Kings, Egypt 6
Giza, Egypt 3
Bermuda Triangle 1, 2
Atlantic Ocean 4, 5

3 Vocabulary practice; practice of simple past verbs (regular and irregular)

- Read the sentences.
- Circle the correct verb in each sentence.

Answers

1	died	4	hit
2	disappeared	5	sank
3	built	6	crashed

Extend your vocabulary (Workbook page 42)
Disasters: drought earthquake fire flood hurricane

➡ Workbook page 42

Grammar

Aims
Present and practice simple past (negative)
Review simple past (affirmative)
Talk about things which are not true in the past

Cultural note
- **The Man in the Iron Mask** is a legend about a prisoner in France in the 17th century. Some people believe that the man was a General in the French army who made King Louis XIV very angry. Louis XIV arrested the General and ordered that he should wear a mask all the time as further punishment.
- **Alexandre Dumas** (1802–1870) is a French writer who wrote many historical novels including *The Vicomte de Bragelonne,* which is based on the legend of The Man in the Iron Mask. In Dumas' story the man in the mask is the King's twin brother.
- **Leonard DiCaprio** (born November 11, 1974) is an American actor. His movies include *Romeo and Juliet*, *Titanic* and *Catch Me If You Can*. In the film *The Man in the Iron Mask*, Leonardo plays King Louis XIV and his identical twin brother.

1 Grammar chart: simple past (negative)

Note:
- We make the simple past negative with subject pronoun + *didn't* + verb, e.g. *I didn't go* NOT ~~*I didn't went.*~~
- We make the simple past negative in the same way for regular and irregular verbs.

See Grammar summary page 108.

2 Controlled practice of simple past (affirmative and negative)
- Read the sentences about the movie *The Man in the Iron Mask*.
- Fill in the sentences with the simple past negative and simple past affirmative of the verbs in parentheses.

Answers
1 didn't play, played
2 didn't want, wanted
3 didn't help, helped
4 didn't love, loved

3 Controlled practice of simple past (negative)
- Look at the pictures.
- Make the sentences negative.

Answers
1 The man in the mask didn't live in a castle in France.
2 He didn't show his face to people in public places.
3 He didn't travel by horse.
4 His brother Louis XIV didn't help him.
5 The man in the mask didn't die in his house.

Finished?
Fast finishers can do Puzzle 10B on page 101.

Answers
hit meet see crash run break
It sank!

Over to you!

4 Personalization; written and oral practice of simple past (negative).
- Read the phrases in the box.
- Write sentences using the simple past (negative) about things you didn't do last night.
- Take turns to tell the class.

Possible answers
I didn't study for an exam.
I didn't sleep well.
I didn't eat a big meal.
I didn't do my homework.
I didn't have extra classes.
I didn't read a book.
I didn't write letters.
I didn't take photos.
I didn't cook.

Extra activity (stronger classes)

Further practice of simple past (affirmative, negative and *yes / no* questions)

This game is motivating for students asking questions and answering them.
- Choose a student to demonstrate the activity on.
- Ask the student a questions in the simple past but tell them they cannot say either *Yes* or *No* in their answer, e.g.
  T: *Did you watch TV yesterday?*
  S1: *I watched TV yesterday.*
  Invite other students to ask questions, e.g.
  S2: *Did you buy anything at the weekend?*
  S1: *I didn't buy anything at the weekend.*
- After ten questions or when a students has said *Yes / No* or made a mistake, change roles.

➡ **Workbook page 43**
➡ **Mixed Ability Worksheets page 21**

Living English

Aims

Read a real life mystery
Read a text quickly to get a general idea about its content
Listen to a profile of a famous piano player
Complete a profile from a listening text
Ask and answer about what you did yesterday
Use intonation in *wh-* questions

Reading

 **Audio CD 2 track 31**

Warm-up

Look at the photo of the "Piano man" and his drawing. What do students think the story is about? In pairs, give students a few minutes to discuss their ideas. Ask pairs to explain their theories.

1 Pre-reading task

- Read the reading skills box.

Reading skills: Getting the general idea
Reading a text quickly helps students:
- get the general idea of its content;
- be better prepared for reading a text in detail.

2 Global comprehension task (first reading)

- Read the article quickly.
- Answer the question.
- Compare answers with the ideas students had in the warm-up.

Answer

The Piano Man is a man who two police officers found on a beach in England. He didn't know his name but he could play the piano very well.

3 Detailed comprehension task (second reading)

- Read the questions.
- Read the article again.
- Answer the questions.

Answers

1 He was from Germany.
2 They found him on a beach near Sheerness in England.
3 They took him to a hospital.
4 Because he played the piano for many hours.
5 Yes, he did.

Listening

Cultural note

- **David Helfgott** (born May 19, 1947) is an Australian piano player whose life was the basis of the 1996 film *Shine*.

1 Comprehension of listening text (first listening)

- Read the chart.
- Listen and fill in the chart.

Audio CD 2 track 32

David Helfgott was born in Melbourne, Australia in 1947. At the age of six, he began playing the piano. He played very well and he wanted to be a pianist. In 1966, at the age of nineteen, he went to London to study music. At this time, he became mentally ill.

In 1970, he returned to Australia and spent some years in hospital. In the 1980s, he started to play the piano professionally and he played in concerts in Japan, Germany and London. His life story was made into a movie called *Shine*. The movie won an Oscar award and made him popular all around the world.

Answers

Name	David Helfgott
Nationality	Australian
Occupation	Pianist

2 Detailed comprehension of listening text (second listening)

- Read the sentences.
- Listen to the profile again.
- Circle the correct words in the sentences.

Answers

1 1947	4 nineteen
2 six	5 movie
3 London	6 was

Speaking

1 First listening

- Look at the pictures and read the model dialog quickly.
- Listen and read.

Audio CD 2 track 33

2 Presentation of pronunciation point

Pronunciation: Intonation in questions

- Our voice usually goes up at the end of *yes / no* questions.

- Read the examples in the Pronunciation box.
- Listen to the examples and repeat, copying the intonation.

Audio CD 2 track 34

3 Pronunciation practice

- Read and practice the questions, going up at the end of each question.
- Listen, check and repeat.

Audio CD 2 track 35

4 Dialog practice

- Practice the model dialog with another student.
- Change roles and practice again.

5 Dialog personalization and practice

- Look at the words in blue in the model dialog.
- Think of some different activities.
- Replace the blue words with your ideas to make a new dialog.
- Practice the dialog with another student.

➡ **Tests page 20**

5 Review

1
1 by plane
2 by boat
3 on foot
4 by train
5 by ship
6 by car

2
1 river
2 desert
3 beach
4 island
5 jungle
6 mountain

3
1 mountains
2 desert
3 rivers
4 beaches
5 island
6 jungle

4
1 crashed
2 disappeared
3 broke
4 hit, sank

Grammar

1
1 moved
2 traveled
3 played
4 arrived
5 stayed
6 learned

2
1 went
2 met
3 gave
4 built
5 spent
6 saw
7 told
8 ran

3
1 When did the Andrea Doria sink?
2 did it sink
3 did it hit the Stockholm
4 did the captain of the Andrea Doria tell people
5 did the captain of the Stockholm take

4
1 He didn't go to school in Boston. He went to school in New York.
2 He didn't play baseball in high school. He played soccer.
3 He didn't work as an artist after high school. He worked as a builder.
4 Later, he didn't work as a singer. He worked as a model.
5 He didn't act in the film *The Rain*. He acted in the film *The Fog*.

Study skills

1
1 Simple present
2 *can*
3 Simple past
4 Present progressive

11 A good idea?

Unit summary

Active vocabulary

- requests: borrow, buy, drive, dye, get, go, have, stay out
- places: amusement park, coffee shop, library, park, museum, shopping mall, skating rink, swimming pool

Passive vocabulary

- nouns: bowling, date, exhibition, fun, grades, idea, sleep-over, storyteller, tattoo
- verbs: decide, invite, Let's
- adjectives: cute, responsible

Grammar

- *can* (permission)
- suggestions

Skills

- Reading letters about problems in a teen magazine; looking for keywords or phrases in a text to help with comprehension
- Writing an e-mail about future plans
- Making and responding to suggestions; identifying and using intonation in responses to suggestions

Cross-curricular

- geography

Values

- ethics and citizenship

Exploring the topic

Vocabulary

Aims

Present and practice verbs for requests
Model *Can I / we ... ?* for permission
Model responses to requests

Warm-up

- Books closed. Which things do students need to ask their parents' permission to do?

1 Presentation of vocabulary set: requests; exposure to requests and answers to requests

- Read the words in the box.
- Fill in the sentences with the correct verbs.
- Listen, check and repeat.

Answers / Audio CD 2 track 36

1 Can we go to a party on Saturday?
2 Can we have a sleep-over?
3 Can I get a tattoo on my arm?
4 Can I borrow some money?
5 Can I dye my hair pink?
6 Can I buy that dog?
7 Can I stay out late tonight?
8 Can I drive the new car to the beach?

2 Practice of responses to requests

- Read the responses to the requests. Which are positive? (*Sure, you can*) Which are negative? (*I'll think about it. / Absolutely not! / No way!*)
- Read the requests in exercise 1 again.
- Think about how your parents would reply to each request.
- Write the number of the request next to the replies.
- Listen and repeat.

Answers / Audio CD 2 track 37

a Sure you can
b I'll think about it
c Absolutely not! No way!

Answers

Students' own answers

Extend your vocabulary (Workbook page 44)

Requests:	go clubbing	go fishing
go shopping	go skiing	go snowboarding
go swimming		

➡ **Workbook page 44**

Grammar

Aims

Present and practice *can* (permission)
Present and practice responses to requests
Ask for permission

1 Grammar chart: *can* (permission)

Note:

- We use *Can I / we / he / she …?* to ask for permission.
- We can use *Yes, you / he / she can*. or *No, you / he / she can't* as responses. Some more natural responses include: *Sure you can. / I'll think about it. / Sorry, you can't. / Absolutely not! No way!*

See Grammar summary page 108.

2 Exposure to asking for and giving / refusing permission

- Read the questions and answers.
- Match each question with the correct answer.

Answers

1 E 2 D 3 A 4 C 5 B

3 Controlled practice of *can* (permission) and appropriate responses

- Look at the pictures.
- Write questions asking for permission with *Can I …?*
- Complete the answers.

Answers

1 Can we have a party?
No you can't.
2 Can I have some cake?
Sorry, you can't.
3 Can I go swimming?
Absolutely not!
4 Can I listen to a CD?
Sure you can
4 Can we play video games?
I'll think about.

Finished?

Fast finishers can do Puzzle 11A on page 101.

Answers

	Nick	Tim	Brad	Jen
drive the car borrow some		✓	✗	✗
money dye his / her	✓	✓	✓	✗
hair	✗	✗	✓	✗
have a party				✓
get a tattoo	✓		✗	
stay out late	✓		✓	✓

Brad can dye his hair and stay out late.

Over to you!

4 Personalization; oral practice of asking for and refusing permission

- Take turns to ask your partner for permission to do something.
- Refuse permission using *Sorry, you can't.*
- Give reasons using the phrases in the box (see example).

➡ Workbook page 45
➡ Mixed Ability Worksheets page 22

Building the topic

Vocabulary

Aims
Present and practice places in a town
Model *Let's … / What about …? / Why don't we …?* for making suggestions
Review infinitive and *-ing* forms.

Warm-up

- Look at the photos. Which of these places do students usually go to at weekends? What do they do there? Which is their favourite place? Elicit the names of the places.

1 Presentation of vocabulary set: places; exposure to suggestions

- Read the words in the box.
- Read the dialogs.
- Fill in the dialogs with the correct words in the box.
- Listen, check and repeat.

Answers / Audio CD 2 track 38

1 skating rink
2 shopping mall
3 park
4 museum
5 swimming pool
6 amusement park
7 library
8 coffee shop

2 Vocabulary practice

- Read and listen to the dialogs.
- Listen and repeat.

Audio CD 2 track 39

3 Vocabulary practice

- Read the statements.
- Read the words in the box in exercise 1 again.
- Write the correct place next to each statement.

Answers

1 amusement park	5 library
2 skating rink	6 coffee shop
3 shopping mall	7 swimming pool
4 museum	8 park

Extend your vocabulary (Workbook page 46)

Opinions:	crazy	great	hate	love
not bad	OK	stand	terrible	

➡ **Workbook page 46**

Grammar

Aims

Present and practice *Let's … / What about …? / Why don't we …?* for suggestions
Present and practice responses for suggestions
Make suggestions

1 Grammar chart: suggestions

Note:

- We use *Let's … / What about …? / Why don't we …?* to make suggestions.
- We use *Let's* + verb, e.g. *Let's play tennis.*
- We use *What about* + *-ing* form, e.g. *What about playing tennis?*
- We use *Why don't we* + verb, e.g. *Why don't we play tennis?*
- We can say *Yes / No* to respond to suggestions but some more natural responses include: *O.K. / That's a good idea. / I don't think so. / Let's not. / No way!*

See Grammar summary page 108.

2 Controlled practice of common structures for making suggestions

- Read the sentences.
- Circle the correct form of the verb for each suggestion.

Answers

1	watching	3	have
2	eat	4	inviting

3 Controlled practice of making suggestions

- Read the phrases in the box.
- Look at the pictures.
- Complete the suggestions with the correct form of the phrases in the box.

Answers

1 rent a DVD.
2 going swimming?
3 cook some food?
4 playing Scrabble?
5 study for the test.

4 Free practice of making suggestions

- Read the phrases in the box.
- Write suggestions using *Let's … , What about …?, Why don't we …?*
- Use each suggestion type once.
- Write responses for the suggestions.

Possible answers

1 What about watching TV?
O.K.
2 Why don't we go skiing?
Let's not
3 Let's do our homework?
No way!
4 What about buying some new clothes?
That's a good idea.

Finished?

Fast finishers can do Puzzle 11B on page 101.

Answers

skating rink
shopping mall
coffee shop
amusement park
swimming pool

✚ 8 ○ △ 8 ✚ = MUSEUM

Over to you!

5 Personalization; oral practice of suggestions and appropriate responses

- Work in groups of four.
- Read the phrases in the box.
- Take turns to make suggestions and respond appropriately (see example).

➡ Workbook page 46
➡ Mixed Ability Worksheets page 23

Living English

Aims

Read about teenagers' problems and the advice they receive
Look for key words and phrases to help answer comprehension questions
Write an e-mail with suggestions and reasons for future plans
Talk about, make and respond to suggestions
Identify and practice intonation in responses to suggestions

Reading

 **Audio CD 2 track 40**

Warm-up

- Books closed. What do students do when they have a problem? Who do they talk to? Who gives the best advice? What other things can students do when they need advice?

1 Global comprehension task (first reading)

- Read the text quickly.
- Where can you find a text like this?

Answer

2 in a teen magazine

2 Presentation of reading skill

- Read the reading skills box.

Reading skills: Looking for key words and phrases
Looking for key words and phrases in a text helps students to:
- read texts more quickly;
- find the answers to comprehension questions more quickly and accurately.

3 Detailed comprehension task (second reading)

- Read the statements.
- Read the article again.
- Circle T (True) or F (False).

Answers

1 F 2 F 3 T 4 F 5 T 6 T 7 F 8 F

Extra activity (all classes)

Review simple present (affirmative and negative)

- Further practice of grammar through correcting false sentences.
- Ask students to correct the false sentences in exercise 3.
- Students write sentences adding explanation if necessary.

Answers

1 James isn't a good student because his grades aren't very good.
2 He isn't on the soccer team at the moment.
4 Anabel's parents don't know the boy, but they don't want Anabel to date until she's 16.
7 Kelly isn't angry with her friends. She's angry with her parents.
8 Wendy thinks fifteen is too young for a tattoo.

Writing

1 Model writing text

- Read the e-mail quickly.
- Answer the question.

Answers

It's about things they can do when Rachel visits Abigail.

2 Detailed analysis of model writing text

- Read the chart.
- Fill in the columns labeled "Suggestion" and "Reason" with information from Abigail's letter.

Answers

Suggestion	Reason
take bus to New York City	not far, a lot to do
go ice-skating on lake	lots of kids go there, it's really fun
go to see Abigail's grandparents	they live in an amazing place

3 Preparation for personalized writing

- Imagine a friend is going to visit you.
- Fill in the columns labeled "You" with your own ideas of suggestions of things to do and reasons to do them.

4 Personalized writing

- Follow the model writing text.
- Use your own ideas from the chart.
- Write an e-mail to your friend.

Speaking

1 First listening

- Look at the pictures and read the model dialog quickly.
- Listen and read.

Audio CD 2 track 41

2 Presentation of pronunciation point

Pronunciation: Responding to suggestions

- When you make a positive response, your voice usually goes up.
- When you make a negative response, your voice usually goes down.
- Using appropriate intonation helps students sound more natural and encourages people to listen.

- Read the examples in the Pronunciation box.
- Listen to the examples and repeat, copying the intonation.

Audio CD 2 track 42

3 Pronunciation practice

- Listen to the suggestions and the responses.
- Note the intonation used in the responses.
- Write P (for a positive response) and N (for a negative response).

Audio CD 2 track 43

1

A: Why don't we go to the mall?

B: I don't think so. I hate shopping!

2

A: What about going to a movie?

B: Yeah. That's a good idea! What's playing?

3

A: Let's go to the ice rink?

B: But there are always a lot of people there. Let's not. It's no fun.

4

A: Why don't we stay at home and play video games?

B: No way! That's boring.

Answers

1 N 2 P 3 N 4 N

4 Dialog practice

- Practice the model dialog with another student.
- Change roles and practice again.

5 Dialog personalization and practice

- Look at the words in blue in the model dialog.
- Think of some different suggestions and responses.
- Replace the blue words with your ideas to make a new dialog.
- Practice the dialog with another student.

➡ **Tests page 22**

12 Alternative travel

Unit summary

Active vocabulary

- adventure sports: climb, drive, paddle, ride a mountain bike, ride a horse, sail, snorkel, walk
- community work: explore, leave, plant, relax, repair, spend (time in a place), stay

Passive vocabulary

- nouns: ankle socks, capital city, comedies, community work, dramas, gossip kayak, musicals, national park, national team, rainforest, sailor, soldier, tight jeans, tour guide, wildlife reserve
- verbs: combine, complain
- adjectives: colourful, wild

Grammar

- *going to* (affirmative, negative and questions)

Skills

- Review of vocabulary and grammar in a board game

Cross-curricular

- geography, sport

Values

- ethics and citizenship, environment

Exploring the topic

Vocabulary

Aims

Present and practice adventure sports
Model *going to* (affirmative)

Cultural note

- **Fiji** is a series of islands in the South Pacific Ocean. There are about 322 islands in total and people live on 106 of them. The capital is Suva and the population is about 900,000 people.
- **The Mamanuca Islands** in Fiji are a series of about twenty volcanic islands.
- **Tanzania** is a country on the east coast of Africa. Its capital is Dar es Salaam and its population is about 37.5 million. Its main language is Swahili.
- **Kilimanjaro** is a mountain in Tanzania. At 5,895 metres it is the highest mountain in Africa and the fourth highest in the word.
- **Tarangire National Park** is a national park in Tanzania. It is 2,600 square kilometres in area and is home to thousands of elephants, leopards, zebras and other wild animals.

Warm-up

- Ask students to imagine they are going on an adventure holiday. What country would they go to? Why? What would they do there? Who would they go with?

1 Presentation of vocabulary set: adventure sports

- Read the verbs and phrases in the box.
- Look at the photos.
- Write the number of the photo next to the verbs and phrases in the box.
- Listen, check and repeat.

Answers / Audio CD 2 track 44

1 ride a mountain bike	5 ride a horse
2 paddle	6 walk
3 snorkel	7 climb
4 sail	8 drive

2 Vocabulary practice; exposure to *going to* (affirmative)

- Read and listen to the statements.
- Read Jeff and Leila's itineraries.
- Circle T (True) and F (False).

Audio CD 2 track 45

Answers

1 F 2 T 3 F 4 F 5 F

Extend your vocabulary (Workbook page 48)

Adventure sports: bungee-jumping hang-gliding parachuting rock-climbing shark diving windsurfing

➡ Workbook page 48

Grammar

Aims
Present and practice *going to* (affirmative)
Talk about future plans and intentions

1 Grammar chart: *going to* (affirmative)

Note:
- We use *going to* to talk about future plans and intentions.
- We make the affirmative form of *going to* with *be* + *going to* + verb

See Grammar summary page 109.

2 Practice of word order of *going to* (affirmative) for plans

- Read the skeleton sentences.
- Put the words in the correct order.

Answers
1 Greg is going to paddle a kayak along the Mississippi river.
2 Sue is going to ride a mountain bike in the Canadian Rockies.
3 Baiko is going to sail a boat along the River Nile in Egypt.
4 Thalia is going to snorkel in the ocean in Hawaii.

3 Controlled practice of *going to* (affirmative)

- Read the weekend plans.
- Fill in the sentences with the correct affirmative form of *be* and *going to*

Answers
1 is going to
2 am going to
3 is going to
4 are going to
5 are going to

4 Controlled practice of *going to* (affirmative)

- Read the verbs in the box.
- Fill in the sentences with the correct affirmative form of *be* and *going to* and a verb in the box.

Answers
1 is going to surf
2 is going to listen
3 are going to ski
4 is going to swim
5 are going to play
6 is going to drive

Extra activity (all classes)

Review *going to* (affirmative)

Students negotiate their diaries to find a time when they are both free.
- Students make a list of the days of the week.
- Students complete five days of the week with their plans, e.g. *Monday – play tennis.*
- In pairs, students try to find a time when they can both meet without showing each other their diaries, e.g.
  S1: *Can you meet me on Monday?*
  S2: *Sorry, no. I'm playing tennis. What about Wednesday?*
  S1: *Sorry. I'm …*
- Students tell the class when they are going to meet, e.g. *Maria and I are going to meet on Friday.*
- Students write sentences adding explanation if necessary.

Finished?
Fast finishers can do Puzzle 12A on page 102.

Answers
Benjamin and Clive are going to climb.
William and Kath are you go walk.
Dave and Irene are going to drive.

Over to you!

5 Personalization; written and oral practice of *going to* (affirmative)

- Read the ideas.
- Write four sentences about your perfect vacation.
- Take turns to tell the class about your plans.

Possible answers
go to – I'm going to Hawaii.
travel by – I'm going to travel by helicopter.
Take my – I'm going to take my MP3 player and swimming costume.
activities / sports – I'm going to play volleyball on the beach.

➡ **Workbook page 49**
➡ **Mixed Ability Worksheets page 24**

Building the topic

Vocabulary

Aims

Present and practice community work verbs
Model *going to* (negative, questions and short answers)
Review *going to* (affirmative)

Cultural note

- **Costa Rica** is a country in Central America. Its capital is San José and its population is about 4 million. Its main language is Spanish. Costa Rica has a good record of environmental protection. National parks cover over 25% of the country.

Warm-up

What is the most exciting trip students have been on? Where did they go? What did they do there? Would they go there again? Have students ever been on a working holiday? What do they think it is? Where would they go if they went on a working holiday? Who would they like to help?

1 Presentation of vocabulary set: community work

- Read the verbs in the box.
- Look at the photos.
- Write the numbers of the photos next to the correct verbs.
- Listen, check and repeat.

Answers / Audio CD 2 track 46

1 spend 2 plant 3 stay
4 repair 5 leave 6 explore
7 relax

2 Vocabulary practice; exposure to *going to* (affirmative, negative, questions and short answers)

- Read the questions.
- Read the text about Pete and Tanya.
- Write P (Pete), T (Tanya) or PT (Pete and Tanya).

Audio CD 2 track 47

Answers

1 PT 2 T 3 PT 4 P 5 PT 6 PT

Extend your vocabulary (Workbook page 50)

Holidays: activity vacation camping vacation cruise hiking vacation safari sightseeing tour

➡ **Workbook page 50**

Grammar

Aims

Present and practice *going to* (questions and short answers)
Present and practice *going to* (negative)
Review *going to* (affirmative)
Talk and ask about future plans

1 Grammar chart: *going to* (questions and short answers)

Note:
- We make *yes / no* questions with going to by swapping the subject pronoun and the auxiliary verb *be*, e.g. *Are you going to the party?*
- We make short answers with *Yes / No* + subject pronoun + the verb *be*. We do not use another verb in short answers, e.g. *Are you going to leave? Yes, I am. / No, I'm not.* NOT ~~*Yes, I am going*~~. or ~~*No, I'm not going.*~~
- We make *wh-* questions by adding a *wh-* word to the *yes / no* question present progressive (*wh-* questions) with question word + *be* + subject + *-ing* form.

See Grammar summary page 109.

2 Controlled practice of *going to* (questions and short answers)

- Complete the questions with the correct form of *be* and *going* to and the verb in parentheses.
- Look at the weather forecast.
- Complete the short answers.

Answers

1 Are we going to sail on a boat on Monday?
No, we aren't.
2 Are we going to visit museums?
Yes, we are.
3 Is the tour guide going to come with us?
Yes, he is.
4 Is Marcos going to explore the jungle on Tuesday?
Yes, he is.
5 Are you going to surf on Wednesday?
Yes, I am.

3 Controlled practice of *going to* (*wh-* questions)

- Read Matt and Liv's plans.
- Write *wh-* questions about Matt and Liv's plans using the information in the answers.

Answers

1 What are Matt and Liv going to do on Monday?
2 Who is going to come with them?
3 Where are they going to relax on Tuesday?
What are they going to do on Tuesday?
4 What are they going to do on Thursday?

4 Grammar chart: *going to* (negative)

Note:
- We make the negative form of *going to* with *be* + not + *going to* + verb.

See Grammar summary page 109.

5 Controlled practice of *going to* (negative)

- Read the sentences about Matt and Liv's future plans.
- Rewrite the sentence in the negative form of *going to*

Answers

1 Liv isn't going to relax on a beach on Saturday.
2 Matt isn't going to paddle in a kayak on Sunday.
3 Matt and Liv aren't going to watch a video about the trip on Sunday.
4 They aren't going to take a lot of photos on Sunday.

Finished?

Fast finishers can do Puzzle 12B on page 102.

Answers

We are going to explore the islands and relax on the beach.

Over to you!

6 Personalization; written and oral practice of *going to* (affirmative, questions and short answers)

- Write three plans for next weekend, using *going to* (affirmative)
- Take turns to ask and answer in class (see example).

➡ **Workbook page 51**
➡ **Mixed Ability Worksheets page 25**

Living English

Aims
Review grammar and vocabulary from the course through a game

Review

Preparation

- Play the game in groups of three or four.
- For each group you need: a dice, a different counter for each player (e.g. a coin)

Rules

- Roll the dice to see who goes first.
- The highest number starts and then the next highest is second, etc.
- On most squares there are instructions.
- Follow the instructions. If you are correct, you move forward to another square. If you are incorrect, you move back one square.
- If there are no instructions, stay on the square and the dice passes to the next player.
- The first player to get to square 26 is the winner.

Possible answers

1 Can you swim?
2 They are watching TV right now.
3 I listen to rap music. I don't listen to classical music.
5 T-shirt, trousers, sneakers, jersey, skirt
6 I get up at seven o'clock every day.
8 Let's play tennis.
9 B It's mine.
11 My hair is long and dark.
12 How many pens are on your desk?
14 head, shoulder, hand, knee, foot
15 They were born in Mexico City.
17 Is there any food in the classroom?
18 I started / didn't go to school in 1996.
19 I saw Julia yesterday.
21 What did you do last weekend?
22 amusement park, coffee shop, library, park, museum
24 I'm going to visit my grandparents this weekend.
26 Would you like some water?

➡ **Tests page 24**

6 Review

Vocabulary

1
1 drive
2 have
3 dye
4 get
5 borrow
6 buy

2
1 E
2 C
3 B
4 A
5 D

3
1 ride a mountain bike
2 walk
3 paddle
4 snorkel
5 ride a horse
6 climb
7 sail

4
1 spend
2 relax
3 plant
4 stay
5 leave
6 explore
7 repair

Grammar

1
1 Can I stay out
2 Can John eat
3 Can we buy
4 Can I dye
5 Can Tim and James play
6 Can I drive

2
1 go
2 having
3 go
4 watching
5 go
6 drive

3
1 is going to go shopping.
2 are going to climb a mountain.
3 are going to sail a boat.
4 are going to snorkel in the sea.
5 are going to plant some flowers.

4
1 Are you going to repair
2 Are they going to run
3 is Wei spending
4 Michael isn't going to stay
5 Are we going to see
6 Mercedes isn't going to travel

Study skills

Students' own answers

Workbook Answer key

Welcome back

1
1 She
2 He
3 they
4 We
5 It
6 you
7 I

2
1 brother
2 sister
3 father
4 mother
5 grandparents

3
1 is, 'm / am
2 n't / are not
3 'm not / am not
4 is, are
5 n't / is not

4
1 Monday
2 Tuesday
3 Wednesday
4 Thursday
5 Friday
6 Saturday
7 Sunday

5
1 January
2 February
3 March
4 April
5 May
6 June
7 July
8 August
9 September
10 October
11 November
12 December

6
1 Don't be
2 Go
3 Have
4 Don't play
5 Come

7
1 blackboard
2 bookself
3 desk
4 chair
5 backpack
6 door
7 locker

Unit 1

Vocabulary

1
1 dance
2 use
3 act
4 do
5 speak
6 play
7 ride

2
1 run fast
2 windsurf
3 make clothes
4 swim
5 water-ski
6 send a text

Grammar

1
1 c
2 d
3 b
4 a

2
1 can't
2 can
3 can't
4 can
5 can't

3
1 Can Amy and Jose make clothes? No, they can't
2 Can Amy dance? Yes, she can.
3 Can Milo send a text? No, he can't.
4 Can Jose and Milo ride a motorcycle? Yes, they can.

Vocabulary

1
1 short
2 wavy
3 moustache
4 big

2

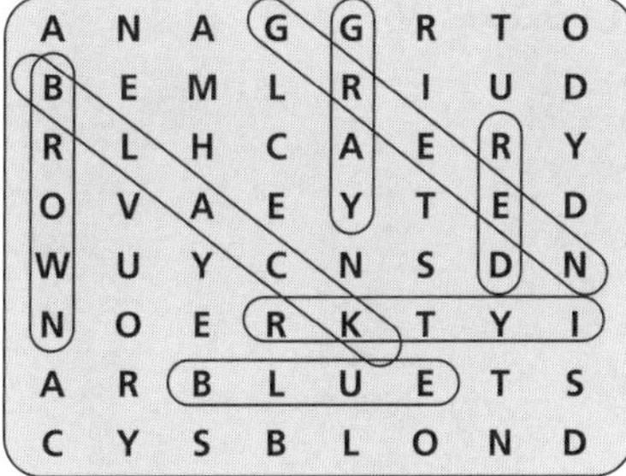

A	N	A	G	G	R	T	O
B	E	M	L	R	I	U	D
R	L	H	C	A	E	R	Y
O	V	A	E	Y	T	E	D
W	U	Y	C	N	S	D	N
N	O	E	R	K	T	Y	I
A	R	B	L	U	E	T	S
C	Y	S	B	L	O	N	D

black
brown
gray
green
red
blue
blond

3
1 short
2 tall
3 curly
4 good-looking
5 dark brown
6 slim
7 overweight
8 strong
9 bald

Grammar

1
1 is, has
2 have
3 's / is
4 has
5 're / are
6 's / is
7 have

2
1 doesn't have
2 isn't
3 don't have
4 aren't

3
1 isn't short, is tall.
2 doesn't have, short hair
3 isn't slim. 's overweight
4 He doesn't have a beard. He has a moustache.
5 They don't have black hair. They have gray hair.

Unit 2

Vocabulary

1
1 c
2 a
3 d
4 b

2
1 carry
2 dance
3 watch
4 sit
5 sing
6 walk
7 swim
8 sunbath
9 celebrate

3
1 It's foggy.
2 It's stormy.
3 It's cloudy.
4 It's freezing.

Grammar

1
1 writing
2 running
3 getting
4 singing
5 celebrating
6 sending

2
1 isn't
2 am
3 are
4 aren't
5 are

3
1 're having
2 's playing
3 's singing
4 're dancing
5 're making
6 're sitting
7 isn't raining
8 'm not doing

Vocabuarly

1
1 is getting
2 waiting
3 talking
4 eating
5 doing
6 babysitting
7 sleeping

2
1 C
2 A
3 D
4 E
5 B

Grammar

1
1 Where are you going?
2 Is your friend watching TV?
3 What is he doing?
4 Are they getting dressed?
5 Is Maria washing her face?

2
1 No, he isn't.
2 Yes, they are.
3 Yes, I am.
4 No, it isn't.
5 Yes, she is.
6 No, we aren't.

3
1 are you doing
2 you reading
3 I'm not
4 your sister doing
5 she isn't
6 Are your mom and dad sitting
7 No, they aren't.
8 Is your brother sleeping?
9 No, he isn't.
10 Is the sun shining?
11 it is.

Unit 3

Vocabulary

1
1 hate
2 speak(s)
3 eat
4 live(s)
5 listen
6 wear
7 teach(es)
8 love

2
1 go
2 take
3 like
4 enjoy
5 learn
6 meet
7 drink

Grammar

1
1 meet
2 gets
3 speak
4 do
5 enjoys
6 dance

2
1 doesn't
2 doesn't
3 don't
4 doesn't
5 doesn't
6 don't

3
1 doesn't like
2 lives
3 plays
4 doesn't like
5 live
6 don't speak
7 loves
8 doesn't live

Vocabulary

1
1 jacket
2 sweatshirt
3 T-shirt
4 sneakers / socks
5 shorts
6 cap
7 jersey

2
1 coat
2 belt
3 gloves
4 scarf
5 bathing suit
6 sandals
7 sunglasses
8 hat

Grammar

1
1 Do, do
2 Do, do
3 Does, does
4 Do, do
5 Does, does
6 Does, doesn't
7 Do, do
8 Do, don't
9 Does, doesn't

2
1 Do you play
2 I do
3 your sister like
4 she doesn't
5 Do your parents go
6 They don't
7 Does Eva wear
8 she doesn't
9 Do you eat
10 No, I don't.
11 Does Delia ride
12 Yes, she does.

Unit 4

Vocabulary

1
1 build
2 cook
3 fix
4 fly
5 program
6 report
7 study

2
1 sell
2 cut
3 save
4 explain
5 fight

Grammar

1
1 works
2 sell
3 builds
4 teaches
5 live
6 flies

2
1 are studying
2 is explaining
3 are listening
4 isn't fixing
5 is swimming
6 is sunbathing

Vocabulary

1

H	R	X	U	G	R	E	B	S
A	W	C	L	E	A	N	Q	T
V	T	G	O	T	O	B	E	D
E	A	C	L	U	P	L	A	Y
S	L	E	E	P	T	A	V	O
D	K	A	S	R	I	D	E	M

1 get up
2 ride
3 have
4 talk
5 go to bed
6 play
7 clean
8 sleep

2
1 do
2 make
3 do
4 do
5 make
6 make

Grammar

1
1 usually
2 right now
3 usually
4 right now
5 right now
6 usually
7 usually
8 right now

2
1 goes
2 is talking
3 clean
4 are having
5 visit
6 is waiting

3
1 go
2 are celebrating
3 are having
4 watch
5 are eating
6 wear
7 am wearing

Unit 5

Vocabulary

1
1 chair
2 bottle
3 glass
4 plate
5 napkin
6 menu
7 person
8 waiter
9 insect
10 table
Restaurant

2
1 knife
2 fork
3 spoon
4 jug
5 bowls
6 cups

Grammar

1
1 is
2 an
3 are
4 spoons
5 some
6 any
7 is

2
1 There is a bowl.
2 There are some cups.
3 There isn't a jug.
4 There aren't any forks.
5 There are some spoons.

3 1 Is there a clock? Yes, there is.
2 Are there any chairs? No, there aren't.
3 is the a CD player? Yes, there is.
4 Are there any posters? Yes there are.
5 Is there a table? No, there isn't.

Vocabulary

1 1 oil
2 water
3 cheese
4 French fries
5 apple
6 bread
7 ketchup
8 salt
9 coffee
10 soda
11 banana
12 sausage

2 1 sandwich
2 salad
3 fruit juice
4 soup
5 orange
6 milk

Grammar

1 1 singular: apple, hamburger, orange, cup, chair
2 plural: apples, spoons, people, books, oranges
3 uncountable: soup, bread, milk, cheese, water,

2 1 any
2 an
3 some
4 any
5 any, some
6 a

3 1 some water
2 a banana
3 There are some books
4 a menu
5 any apples
6 There isn't any bread
7 any people
8 a teacher
9 There is some milk

Unit 6

Vocabulary

1 1 hand
2 arm
3 neck
4 leg
5 foot
6 ear
7 head
8 eye
9 nose
10 mouth

2 A eyebrows
B lips
C teeth
D fingers
E thumb
F nails

Grammar

1 1 is, It's
2 these, They're
3 this, It's
4 are, They're

2 1 d
2 e
3 a
4 f
5 b
6 c

3 1 Whose watch is this?
2 It's hers.
3 Whose, these
4 theirs
5 Whose jacket, this?
6 It's his.
7 Whose magazines are these?
8 They're mine.

Vocabulary

1 1 heavy
2 new
3 expensive
4 slow
5 noisy
6 soft

2 1 boring, interesting
2 difficult, easy
3 beautiful, ugly
4 wet, dry
5 hardworking, lazy

Grammar

1 1 F
2 T
3 F
4 F
5 T
6 T

2 1 Serena loves beautiful cities.
2 Kimio's hair is short and black.
3 Serena has big blue eyes.
4 Rex is and noisy young dog.
5 Kimio has a small old car

3 1 long, blond hair
2 expensive new computer
3 a lazy old dog
4 is small and old
5 computer is cheap

Unit 7

Vocabulary

1 1 d
2 f
3 g
4 a
5 c
6 b
7 h
8 e

2 1 department store
2 road sign
3 sky scraper
4 billboard
5 stop light
6 sidewalk

Grammar

1
1 much
2 many
3 much
4 many
5 many
6 much

2
1 is
2 aren't
3 a few
4 are
5 a little
6 isn't

3
1 How, furniture
2 isn't much
3 How, cars
4 lot of
5 How many people are
6 There aren't many
7 Is there much baggage in the hall?
8 There's a lot of baggage in the hall.
9 Is there much food in the refrigerator?
10 There isn't much food in the refrigerator.

Vocabulary

1
1 rice
2 chicken
3 muffins
4 apples
5 ice cream
6 yogurt
7 juice
8 toothpaste
9 paper towel
10 soap

2
1 potatoes
2 shampoo
3 steak
4 toothbrush
5 tomatoes
6 grapes

Grammar

1
1 Would you like some juice?
2 Would you like some ice cream?
3 Would you like some money?
4 Would you like a banana?
5 Would you like some shampoo?
6 Would you like a toothbrush?

2
1 I'd like some steak.
2 He'd like a banana.
3 We'd like some fruit juice.
4 She'd like a yogurt.
5 They'd like some grapes.

3
1 Would you like
2 Would you like an, a
3 I'd like
4 Would you like some
5 Would you like a
6 That'd be

Unit 8

Vocabulary

1

O	P	E	F	A	C	S	O	G	Y	K
S	O	N	G	W	R	I	T	E	R	A
U	L	E	U	K	O	D	I	A	R	D
P	I	B	I	N	V	E	N	T	O	R
E	T	S	T	U	Q	S	A	O	G	U
B	I	R	A	R	T	I	S	T	U	N
Y	C	E	R	X	A	G	R	E	P	N
W	I	M	I	S	H	N	J	I	T	E
P	A	C	S	O	L	E	A	D	E	R
I	N	O	T	V	E	R	P	E	C	L

1 artist
2 inventor
3 guitarist, songwriter
4 leader, politician
5 runner, designer

2
1 movie director
2 explorer
3 queen
4 racing driver
5 composer
6 author

Grammar

1
1 weren't, Were
2 was
3 wasn't
4 Was, wasn't
5 were
6 Were

2
1 wasn't, was
2 were, was
3 wasn't
4 weren't, were

3
1 Were
2 I was
3 was
4 Were you
5 I wasn't
6 I was
7 Were
8 they were
9 were
10 It was

Vocabulary

1
1 happy
2 sad
3 nervous
4 tired
5 surprised
6 bored
7 scared

2
1 excited
2 sick
3 disappointed
4 worried
5 jealous

Grammar

1
1 fourth
2 two
3 eleventh
4 fifteen
5 third
6 twenty-four
7 first

2
1 fifth
2 second
3 Christopher
4 sixth
5 first
6 Martin
7 third

3
1 seven
2 first
3 eleven
4 seventh
5 twenty-four

Unit 9

Vocabulary

1
1 foot
2 car
3 boat
4 ship
5 plane
Train

2
1 van
2 truck
3 kayak
4 yacht
5 helicopter
6 subway train

Grammar

1
1 washed
2 stopped
3 moved
4 carried
5 traveled

2
1 lived
2 dropped
3 cooked
4 danced
5 tried
6 used

3
1 walked
2 arrived
3 studied
4 played
5 started
6 finished
7 visited
8 watched

Vocabulary

1
1 gave
2 built
3 met
4 ran
5 went
6 told
7 spent
8 saw

2
1 got up
2 rode
3 came
4 did
5 sent

Grammar

1
1 past
2 present
3 present
4 past
5 present
6 past
7 past
8 present
9 past

2
1 went
2 sent
3 got up
4 did
5 met
6 saw
7 spent
8 came

Unit 10

Vocabulary

1
1 desert
2 beach
3 river
4 jungle
5 mountain
6 island

2
1 lake(s)
2 waterfall(s)
3 volcano
4 cave(s)
5 rainforest

Grammar

1
1 Where did Steve and his sister go last Saturday?
2 When did the match start?
3 Who did they visit?
4 Did they eat some grapes?
5 What did they eat at grandpa's house?
6 What did they do in the evening?

2
1 he did.
2 they didn't.
3 Yes, they did.
4 Yes, he did.
5 No, he didn't.

3
1 Why did you go
2 How did you travel?
3 When did you arrive?
4 Did, win
5 What did you do
6 Did you go

Vocabulary

1

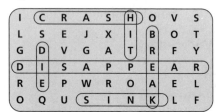

I	C	R	A	S	H	O	V	S
L	S	E	J	X	I	B	O	T
G	D	V	G	A	T	R	F	Y
D	I	S	A	P	P	E	A	R
R	E	P	W	R	O	A	E	L
O	Q	U	S	I	N	K	L	F

1 sink
2 hit
3 break
4 disappear
5 die
6 crash

2
1 drought
2 hurricane
3 earthquake
4 flood
5 fire

Grammar

1
1 My parents didn't watch the movie.
2 You didn't wear your coat.
3 We didn't buy any milk.
4 My sister didn't break that plate.
5 I didn't see the fire.
6 The car didn't crash into the tree.
7 The boat didn't sink in the hurricane.

2
1 She didn't go to the clothes store.
She went to the music store.
2 She didn't buy three books. She bought three CDs.
3 She didn't spend $200. She spent $20.
4 Terry and Bria didn't have lunch at 1:00. They had lunch at 12:00.
5 Bria didn't play the guitar in the afternoon. She played the piano.
6 She didn't watch a soccer game in the evening. She watched a baseball game.

Unit 11

Vocabulary

1
1 get
2 dye
3 stay out
4 borrow
5 drive
6 have
7 buy
8 go

2
1 go shopping
2 go skiing
3 go clubbing
4 go snowboarding
5 go fishing
6 go swimming

Grammar

1
1 A: Can we go to the beach.
B: Sure you can. It's a beautiful day.
2 A: Can we go skiing in Switzerland this Christmas?
B: I'll have to think about it, but it's expensive.
3 A: Can Maria drive your sports car?
B: No way! She's too young.
4 A: Can Jose come to the concert with us?
B: Sorry, he can't. There aren't any seats.
5 A: Can we go swimming in the lake?
B: Yes, you can, but be careful – the water is cold.
6 A: Can I borrow your laptop?
B: Sorry, you can't. I'm using it today.

2
1 A: Can I visit, B: you can
2 A: Anna come, B: can
3 A: Can I borrow, B: can't
4 A: Can I go B: you can't
5 A: Can we have B: you can't

Vocabulary

1
1 shop
2 library
3 museum
4 park
5 rink
6 amusement park
7 pool
8 mall

2
1 stand
2 hate
3 It's terrible!
4 OK
5 not bad
6 great
7 love
8 crazy

Grammar

1
1 A: watch B: so
2 A: have B: not
3 A: doing B: No
4 A: go B: a good
5 A: visiting B: think

2
1 Let's go to the amusement park? OK
2 going, don't
3 don't, visit. OK.
4 visiting your cousin, No
5 Let's, a good idea
don't we make a cake, not
7 What about, That's a
8 Let's listen, don't think so

Unit 12

Vocabulary

1
1 sail
2 mountain
3 horse
4 drive
5 walk
6 paddle
7 climb
Snorkel

2
1 hang-gliding
2 rock-climbing
3 bungee-jumping
4 windsurfing
5 parachuting
6 shark diving

Grammar

1
1 Future
2 Past
3 Future
4 Past
5 Future
6 Past
7 Future
8 Future

2
1 'm
2 's / is
3 are
4 'r / are
5 'm / am
6 is
7 are

3
1 going to watch
2 is going to win
3 is going to drive to work
4 are going to play tennis
5 are going to get up

Vocabulary

1

S	P	E	N	D	I	R	L
T	F	L	R	E	C	Y	P
A	L	O	E	P	O	T	H
Y	E	X	P	L	O	R	E
D	A	T	A	A	Q	E	W
O	V	R	I	N	E	L	P
N	E	C	R	T	U	A	Y
Y	M	N	E	P	T	X	O

1 explore
2 Relax
3 plant
4 leave
5 spend
6 repair
7 stay

2
1 cruise
2 sightseeing tour
3 camping holiday
4 safari
5 activity holiday
6 hiking holiday

Grammar

1
1 Is the cruise going to stop in the caribbean?
2 Louisa is going to talk to her friends.
3 Where are we going to stay tonight?
4 When are you going to repair the car?
5 We aren't going to study tomorrow.
6 Tom and Tina aren't going to plant a tree in the yard.
7 I'm not going to enjoy the camping holiday.
8 Dad isn't going to go on the sightseeing tour.

2
1 aren't going to watch
2 isn't going to repair
3 aren't going to go play
4 isn't going to come
5 isn't going to babysit

3
1 are you going to do
2 you going to watch
3 am
4 Claudia going to come
5 she isn't
6 are you going to play
7 Are you going to relax
8 I'm not
9 Are your friends meeting
10 they aren't

Extra Reading 1

1
1 near a forest
2 King of England
3 marry Robin
4 the King's brother

2
1 love
2 poor
3 Robin's
4 tree

3 Students' own answers

Extra reading 2

1
1 having a vacation
2 south
3 exciting

2
1 T
2 F
3 T

3 Students' own answers

Extra reading 3

1
1 India
2 France
3 England

2
1 disliked
2 one child
3 wasn't

3 Students' own answers

Extra reading 4

1
1 c
2 b
3 d
4 a

2
1 surprised
2 sad
3 afraid
4 happy

3 Students' own answers